BFI Film Classics

C000269251

The BFI Film Classics is a series of books that introduces, interprets and celebrates landmarks of world cinema. Each volume offers an argument for the film's 'classic' status, together with discussion of its production and reception history, its place within a genre or national cinema, an account of its technical and aesthetic importance, and in many cases, the author's personal response to the film.

For a full list of titles available in the series, please visit our website: www.palgrave.com/bfi

'Magnificently concentrated examples of flowing freeform critical poetry.'
Uncut

'A formidable body of work collectively generating some fascinating insights into the evolution of cinema.'
Times Higher Education Supplement

'The series is a landmark in film criticism.'
Quarterly Review of Film and Video

'Possibly the most bountiful book series in the history of film criticism.'
Jonathan Rosenbaum, *Film Comment*

The General

Peter Krämer

A BFI book published by Palgrave

For Thomas

First published in 2016 by
PALGRAVE

on behalf of the

BRITISH FILM INSTITUTE
21 Stephen Street, London W1T 1LN
www.bfi.org.uk

There's more to discover about film and television through the BFI. Our world-renowned archive, cinemas, festivals, films, publications and learning resources are here to inspire you.

PALGRAVE in the UK is an imprint of Macmillan Publishers Limited, registered in England, company number 785998, of 4 Crinan Street, London N1 9XW. Palgrave Macmillan in the US is a division of St Martin's Press LLC, 175 Fifth Avenue, New York, NY 10010. Palgrave is a global imprint of the above companies and is represented throughout the world. Palgrave® and Macmillan® are registered trademarks in the United States, the United Kingdom, Europe and other countries.

Series cover design: Ashley Western
Series text design: ketchup/SE14
Images from *The General* (Buster Keaton/Clyde Bruckman, 1926), © Joseph M. Schenck;
Our Hospitality (Buster Keaton/Jack G. Blystone, 1923), © Joseph M. Schenck Productions;
Neighbors (Buster Keaton/Eddie Cline, 1921), © Metro Pictures Corporation; *Fatty at Coney Island* (Roscoe Arbuckle, 1917), Comique Film Corporation; *The Gold Rush* (Charles Chaplin, 1925), © Roy Export S.A.S.; *The Iron Horse* (John Ford, 1924), Fox Film Corporation; *The Hollywood Revue* (Charles F. Riesner, 1929), © Metro-Goldwyn-Mayer/Loew's Incorporated.

Set by couch
Printed in China

This book is printed on paper suitable for recycling and made from fully managed and sustained forest sources. Logging, pulping and manufacturing processes are expected to conform to the environmental regulations of the country of origin.

British Library Cataloguing-in-Publication Data
A catalogue record for this book is available from the British Library
A catalog record for this book is available from the Library of Congress

ISBN 978–1–84457–915–0

Contents

Acknowledgments

As I finish this book in the autumn of 2015, I can look back on thirty years of research on Buster Keaton. The earliest stages of my work on his films took place in the context of an MA in Film Studies at the University of East Anglia in 1985/6. At that time, I was taught and mentored by Thomas Elsaesser, who continued with his guidance for many years afterwards. This book is dedicated to him.

I am also grateful to Kevin Brownlow, who opened his personal archive to me in the late 1980s, to Tom Dardis and Marion Meade, who supported my work in various ways around the same time, and to many archivists in the United States. Henry Jenkins was extraordinarily supportive during my first ever research trip to the United States in 1988, and gave me tremendous help with my first two publications on Keaton. I should also mention a group of dedicated 'Keatonians' who I kept meeting at academic conferences in the United States and the UK over the years, especially Roberta Pearson, Joanna Rapf, Kevin Sweeney, Peter Parshall and Charles Wolfe. They helped me to keep my interest in Keaton alive, even after the focus of my film historical research had shifted to more recent decades. In the last few years, the students on my introductory film history course at UEA have shown a lot of enthusiasm for Keaton's films, which encouraged me to consider writing about them again. Thanks a lot for this! Finally, I wish to thank Joseph Garncarz, Jenna Steventon and especially Lee Grieveson for feedback on my first draft of this book, and to Sophia Contento for her help with the pictures.

Introduction

The comedian Buster Keaton was just over thirty years old when he co-wrote, directed and starred in *The General*. The film was released in February 1927, towards the end of the era of silent cinema in the United States. Its playfully misleading title raises the expectation that

the film focuses on the deeds of a military leader. In fact, *The General* recreates a famous Civil War episode – a daring Northern raid into Southern territory – from the perspective of a Southern civilian, and, unlike the war, the film ends with a catastrophic defeat for the North. *The General* was presented to the American public as a 'comedy spectacle', a phrase repeatedly used in the lavish press book produced by the film's distributor United Artists, and picked up by many journalists.[1]

The American Civil War was not then, and is not now, an obvious subject for comedy. Prompted by the secession of a confederacy of Southern states from the United States of America, the Civil War lasted from 1861 to 1865. At the heart of the conflict was the Southern institution of slavery, which was brought to an end by the North's victory. Over 600,000 soldiers were killed, a number

approximately equal to the total American fatalities in the Revolution, the War of 1812, the Spanish-American War, World War I, World War II, and the Korean War. ... A similar rate, about 2 percent [of the total US population at the time], today would mean six million fatalities.[2]

The Southern states were hit particularly hard: 'one in five white southern men of military age [13–45] did not survive', and a much higher percentage were injured, often severely.[3] The majority of the war's 50,000 civilian deaths also occurred in the South.[4] In both the South and the North, most families were deeply affected by the war, memories of separation, injury and death being carried forward for many generations to come.

In the light of these facts, it is not so surprising that the two films which had the greatest impact on American culture during the first half of the twentieth century both dealt with the Civil War: *The Birth of a Nation* (1915) and *Gone with the Wind* (1939).[5] It *is* surprising, however, that these films show the antebellum South in a positive light – slaves being portrayed as loyal servants or happy plantation workers – and sympathetically focus on the utter devastation the war brought to the Southern states, as well as the desperate struggles of white Southerners in the aftermath of their defeat. Coming halfway between these two – in retrospect rather uncomfortable, even disturbing – film historical milestones, *The General* also takes, it would initially seem, the Southern side.

The film tells the story of Johnnie Gray, a locomotive engineer on the Western and Atlantic Railroad in Marietta, Georgia. According to an expository intertitle, he has 'two loves in his life' – 'his engine', which is called 'General', and his girlfriend Annabelle. When the Civil War breaks out, Annabelle expects Johnnie to enlist, but the general in charge of recruitment decides that he should be turned away, because, in the words of a dialogue intertitle, '[h]e is more valuable to the South as an engineer', a reason no one bothers to convey to Johnnie. In the mistaken belief that he never even tried to enlist, Annabelle's father calls him 'a disgrace to the South', while Annabelle tells Johnnie: 'I don't want you to speak to me again until you are in uniform.'

One year later, '[i]n a Union encampment just North of Chattanooga', General Thatcher plans a raid into the South with his 'chief spy', Captain Anderson. Some time afterwards, Johnnie sees Annabelle saying goodbye to her injured brother and boarding his train in Marietta to visit her father, who has been injured as well. Anderson and his raiding party are also on the train. During a dinner break in Big Shanty, they steal the General. Unbeknownst to Johnnie, the only passenger remaining on the stolen train is Annabelle. To retrieve his beloved engine, Johnnie pursues it on his own, first on foot, then with a handcar, a bicycle and another train (the Texas), moving into enemy territory. When the Northern spies belatedly realise that they are being pursued by just one man, Johnnie abandons the Texas. Wandering around in stormy weather at night, he seeks shelter in a house which turns out to be the headquarters of the Union army. Hidden under a table, he overhears discussions about General Thatcher's plan for a decisive coordinated attack the next day. Union troops and supply trains are to meet at the Rock River bridge: 'Once our trains and troops cross that bridge, nothing on earth can stop us.' In addition to this vital military information, Johnnie also finds out that Annabelle is being held captive.

That same night he liberates her, and the next morning he recaptures the General and races back to his own lines to 'warn them of this coming attack', with the Texas, now in Union hands, in hot pursuit. Along the way, he starts a fire on the Rock River bridge. After alerting the same Southern general who had prevented him from enlisting about the impending attack, he joins the Confederate forces in a borrowed uniform, while Annabelle is

reunited with her father. During the battle at the Rock River bridge, the fire Johnnie has started leads to its collapse when the Texas tries to cross. Johnnie accidentally kills a Northern sniper when the blade of his sword flies off the handle. Also accidentally, he breaches a nearby dam, releasing a huge volume of water into the river, forcing the Union army to retreat. When the victorious Confederate army returns home, Johnnie realises that the officer he knocked out in the cab of his engine during its recapture is General Thatcher. He delivers the Union commander to the Southern general, who then enlists Johnnie as a lieutenant in the Confederate army, with Annabelle and her father looking on. The film ends with Johnnie kissing her, while sitting on the General and saluting Southern troops.

The General is widely regarded as the greatest achievement in Keaton's long career, which took him from being a child star on the vaudeville stage in the early 1900s to appearing in movies from 1917 onwards. From 1920 to 1928, he had his own studio, directing and starring in nineteen short films and ten features (*The General* was number eight). In 1928, the Keaton company was dissolved and the comedian moved to Metro-Goldwyn-Mayer (MGM), where he appeared in ten films until 1933, of which all but the first two were 'talkies'. Afterwards Keaton, although no longer a major star, remained highly active – as a director, performer and consultant, in American and European short and feature films, on television, in circuses and theatres – almost right up to his death at the age of seventy on 1 February 1966. His silent movies were re-released in the 1960s, after which they quickly gathered an enormous reputation, none more so than *The General*.

Today, *The General* has a rather unique status. It is the highest ranked movie from the silent era on the American Film Institute's 2007 list of the one hundred 'greatest American films of all time'.[6] It is also – after the drama *Sunrise* (1927), which was, however, made with a pre-recorded soundtrack (including music and sound effects) – the second highest ranked American movie from the silent era in

Sight & Sound's 2012 survey of international critical opinion about 'the greatest films of all time' (with Keaton's *Sherlock Jr.* [1924] right behind in third place).[7] Crucially, *The General* is also – after Charles Chaplin's *The Kid* (1921) and *The Gold Rush* (1925) – the third highest ranked American film from the silent era on the Internet Movie Database's users' chart.[8] Thus managing to combine accolades from professionals and from regular movie audiences, *The General* is perhaps more successful than any other American film in keeping the silent era alive for today's film viewers.

This could not have been foreseen when *The General* was first shown to American film critics and cinema audiences. While the film received a lot of praise, it was also criticised quite harshly. The trade paper *Variety*, for example, described *The General* as 'a burlesque of a Civil War meller' (that is, melodrama), and noted that, while '[t]here are some corking gags', overall the film simply was not funny enough, mainly because it was 'built on that elementary bit, the chase, and you can't continue a flight for almost an hour and expect results'.[9] What is more, 'the action is placed entirely in the hands of the star. It was his story, he directed, and he acted,' with the unfortunate consequence, in the paper's opinion, that '[n]o one besides the star has a chance to do anything.' The review also pointed out that 'there was far from a heavy play for the picture the first three days of its run' at the Capitol cinema in New York and predicted that it would not do well in 'de luxe houses'.

Newspaper reviewers tended to agree. The *New York Telegram* referred to a press release which declared *The General* to be 'the most expensive comedy ever to see the light on Broadway' and then judged the film to be 'a pretty trite and stodgy piece of screen fare, a rehash, pretentiously garnered, of any old two reel chase-comedy'.[10] In particular, it complained about Keaton's ubiquity in the film: 'he monopolizes the entire picture with his one-expression countenance'. This complaint was shared by the *New York Mirror*, which found one main fault with Keaton's 'expensive Civil War monologue': 'a too pronounced "I" shaping its

destiny. … One wearies of the star's expressionless monologue.'[11]
The paper warned Keaton that 'being the whole show' might
'jeopardize his popularity'.

Pursuing a different line of attack, the *New York Telegraph*
wrote: 'The camera work is good, the settings excellent, the gags
among the funniest we have seen – and yet the piece lacks life.'[12]
The paper offered a possible explanation: 'Perhaps the subject itself
was too tragic to make the humor unrestrained.' According to the
New York Sun, choosing a very serious subject had recently become
common among the leading comics (notably with *The Gold Rush*):
'one more comedian has felt the bitter sting of ambition and
succumbed … to the current epidemic. Buster Keaton, he of the
stony face and immobile mouth, has made an historical drama –
with comic moments.'[13] The film was judged to be only a qualified
success: 'As a drama, *The General* is occasionally exciting, always
well timed, often spectacular. As a comedy it offers meager fare.'
Similarly, the *New York Evening World* noted that, compared to
Keaton's earlier films, *The General* 'tells more of a story, and
Keaton develops more of a characterization'.[14] The problem with
this was seen to be his performance style: 'Buster has not learnt to
smile. His frozen face is an asset in gag comedy, but when he
ventures into character it proves a serious drawback.'

Life also noted 'signs of vaulting ambition' in Keaton's work:
'He appears to be attempting to enter the "epic" class.'[15] This,
according to the review, was a mistake 'due to the scantiness of his
material as compared with the length of the film' and also because
of the seriousness of the subject: 'it is difficult to derive laughter from
the sight of men being killed in battle'; indeed, '[m]any of his gags
at the end of the picture are in such gruesomely bad taste that the
sympathetic spectator is inclined to look the other way.' Another
reviewer mourned Keaton's 'radical departure from the usual slapstick
brand of comedy'.[16] He noted that the film-maker 'tries principally for
spectacular effects' rather than 'the gags which made him famous',
and found the result 'unusually and peculiarly depressing'.

Several reviews mentioned how convincingly and compellingly *The General* evoked the past. The *New York Post*, for example, wrote that Keaton's character looked 'like something out of the old family album in the parlor' and called the film 'a moving daguerreotype'.[17] *Motion Picture Classic* similarly noted: 'Buster, in his make-up, looks like some old-timer in the plush-covered album.'[18] The magazine also pointed out that Keaton had found 'inspiration in an actual incident', which the *Philadelphia Inquirer* identified as '[t]he Andrews Railroad Raid of 1862'.[19]

Taking my cues from the film's initial critical reception as well as its marketing, in this book I take a fresh look at *The General* and Keaton's career up to the late 1920s. In doing so, I complement a detailed and systematic analysis of the film's story, themes and style (the focus of Chapters 5–7) with references not only to the biographical and critical literature on Keaton but also to a wide range of primary sources, many of which have not previously been paid sufficient attention to. These sources relate to Keaton's working methods and the contractual relations framing his output in the 1920s, to the marketing both of *The General* and of Keaton's earlier films, as well as to their critical reception (the focus of Chapters 1–2). I also draw (in Chapters 3–4) on primary sources relating to the production history of *The General*, notably the book it is based upon. In addition, I make use (in Chapters 1–3 and the Conclusion) of financial data to examine the commercial performance of Keaton's films, to compare it with that of the films made by his main competitors (notably Chaplin and Harold Lloyd), and to relate *The General* to dominant trends at the American box office in the mid-1920s.

My aim, then, is to situate *The General* within Keaton's career and to place this career in the context of key developments in American silent cinema. In examining those narrative, thematic and stylistic characteristics which made it difficult for contemporary critics fully to appreciate *The General*, I highlight the very qualities that have, I believe, underpinned the film's celebration by later generations of viewers. These qualities include Keaton's 'frozen face', the film's emotionally detached style and strong emphasis on physical and cognitive processes, as well as its surprisingly ambiguous, indeed downbeat, ending, which articulates a subtle, but forceful critique of military and Southern culture.

1 Family Affairs

In May 1927, while *The General* was still playing in American movie theatres, the leading fan magazine *Photoplay* published an article about Buster Keaton, written by his father, Joe.[20] It told the story of how Buster, born on 4 October 1895 while Joe and his wife Myra were stopping over in Piqua, Kansas, with their travelling medicine show, was presented to the audience the very next day: 'So, Buster Keaton made his first appearance on any stage when he was just twenty-four hours old.'[21] A few years later, Joe Keaton reported, Buster had become a member of the family act, which was a big success in vaudeville: 'Billed as "The Three Keatons", his mother and I had a burlesque acrobatic set in which my wife and I threw Buster about the stage like a human medicine ball.'[22] An anecdote about Joe targeting a 'trouble-maker in the front row' with his son, who 'flattened' the man's nose, suggested that it had been Joe doing the actual throwing.[23] What Joe failed to mention was that, just as he had once incorporated his young son into his stage act, Buster had arranged for his father to appear in some of the films he made with Arbuckle.[24] He had also given Joe parts in his own films, most recently in *The General*, in which he played a Union general who suffers a few falls and gets doused with water.[25]

Familial relations had been absolutely central to Keaton's career.[26] After occasional, earlier stage appearances, in 1901 five-year-old Joseph Frank Keaton, who was advertised as 'Buster', became the featured attraction of the family act, quickly making it a huge success on the major vaudeville circuits. The act focused on a scenario in which tiny Buster interfered with his tall father's attempt to do a presentation for the audience and received physical punishment in return, this punishment being staged in a supremely

acrobatic and at the same time, it appeared, excessively violent
fashion. After 1909, with the child having grown into a teenager
and Joe finding it increasingly difficult (partly due to his alcoholism)
to execute their physically demanding stage routine, 'The Three
Keatons' gradually lost their popularity, and in 1917 Myra Keaton
decided to dissolve the act. Although her son quickly signed a
well-paid contract to appear as a solo act in the Shubert brothers'
prestigious annual stage revue *The Passing Show of 1917* on
Broadway, he then decided instead to join Roscoe Arbuckle's
recently founded Comique Film Corporation. In the preceding years,
Arbuckle, together with other stars such as Chaplin and Mabel
Normand, had demonstrated the enormous, indeed unprecedented,
popularity that slapstick comedians could achieve in the movies,
while physical humour of the kind Keaton specialised in had
become marginal in the theatre, where successful revue acts relied
much more heavily on verbal, musical and dancing skills.

Joe Keaton (foreground right) in *The General*

In addition to continuing the tradition of vaudeville slapstick, the movies in general, and Comique in particular, also appealed to Keaton because, instead of going solo, he would be able to continue to work with others as he had done all his life (indeed, many members of the Comique team had a similar background in vaudeville). What is more, Arbuckle had announced that with Comique he wanted to develop new movie talents, who, having started out as sidekicks to the comedian in his two-reel shorts (a reel of 35mm film being 1,000 feet long and, depending on projection speed, lasting between 10 and 15 minutes), might one day star in their own movies. When, in 1919–20, Arbuckle moved to Paramount to appear in features, Keaton was indeed promoted to be the star of his own series of two-reelers, continuing to work with many of the people on Arbuckle's team, notably the cinematographer Elgin Lessley and the studio manager Lou Anger.

Keaton's production unit, which had its own studio in Hollywood, included the writer Eddie Cline (who was also Keaton's most frequent co-director and acted in several films) and the actors Sybil Seely, Virginia Fox and Joe Roberts, as well as the 'technical director' Fred Gabourie.[27] When Keaton made the transition from shorts to features in 1923 (by which time Comique had been reorganised as Buster Keaton Productions Inc. in the wake of the Arbuckle scandal of 1921–2), he no longer employed a stock company of actors, but Gabourie stayed on until 1928, Anger until 1927[28] and Lessley until 1926, when he was replaced by J. Deveraux Jennings and Bert Haines, who then worked for Keaton until 1928. On his first five features, Keaton collaborated with a trio of writers: Jean Havez (who he knew from his last three films with Arbuckle on which Havez had been employed as a writer), Joseph A. Mitchell and Clyde Bruckman (also the co-writer and co-director of *The General*). On the remaining five Buster Keaton Productions releases, several names appeared repeatedly in the writing credits: Albert Boasberg, Charles Smith and Carl Harbaugh. Furthermore, throughout most of this period, Keaton worked with Denver

Harmon, who was credited for 'electrical' and 'lighting effects'.[29]

At his own studio, then, Keaton (who was not yet twenty-five years old when he was first put in charge in 1920) had a fairly stable production team, who, among other things, served as a kind of substitute family, complementing the frequent appearances in his films of his father and other family members. Joe Keaton played both major and minor roles in three of the first four short films the Keaton studio made – *Convict 13* (1920), *The Scarecrow* (1920), *Neighbors* (1921) – and also in *Daydreams* (1922); furthermore, he appeared in two of its first three features – *Our Hospitality* (1923) and *Sherlock Jr.* – as well as in *Go West* (1925) and *The General*. In *Our Hospitality*, Joe was joined in the cast by Buster's first son (who had been born on 2 June 1922 as Joseph Talmadge Keaton but was credited as 'Buster Keaton Jr.') and Buster's wife.[30]

Joe Keaton not only provided his son with personal continuity between his stage and film careers but also came to represent

Natalie Talmadge Keaton in *Our Hospitality* (1923)

important continuities in the content of his work. Joe and Buster
engage in acrobatic fights, like the ones they had previously
executed on stage, in the Arbuckle short films *A Country Hero*
(1917)[31] and *The Bell Boy* (1918),[32] and in *Neighbors*. What is
more, in the latter film, Buster and Joe play a misbehaving son and
a father doling out violent punishment, thus recreating the basic
scenario of their stage act. The difference is that in *Neighbors* the
father's objective is to prevent his son's romance. The theme of
paternal interference with a young man's love is picked up in *The
Scarecrow* and *Daydreams*, in which Joe plays the father of the
young woman Buster's character falls for (I shall refer to her in the
parlance of the day as 'the girl'), once again trying to prevent their
romance, with more or less violent means.[33]

Buster Keaton also focused on the mostly rather contentious
relationship between the young protagonist and the girl's father,
here played by other actors (usually Joe Roberts), in *Convict 13*,

Joe and Buster Keaton in *Neighbors* (1921)

The Haunted House (1921), *The High Sign* (1921), *The Goat* (1921), *My Wife's Relations* (1922) and *The Electric House* (1922). Thus, in many of his short films, Keaton developed variations of the theme that had dominated the first fifteen years of his career on stage: the conflict between father and son. It is no coincidence, then, that *The Saphead*, a 1920 Metro feature he appeared in to help launch his career as a movie star in his own right (rather than as Arbuckle's sidekick), tells the story of a young man whose romance with the girl he loves is blocked by his father, who is also the girl's guardian.

This pattern came to dominate Buster Keaton Productions' features, despite the fact that the story ideas for these films came from many different sources, rather than just springing from Keaton's head. Both *Seven Chances* (1925) and *Battling Butler* (1926) were based on stage plays, while *Three Ages* (1923) – with its three parallel stories set in the Stone Age, Roman times and contemporary America – echoed Griffith's *Intolerance* (1916) and other films from the 1910s and 20s featuring two or more stories set in different periods. *Sherlock Jr.* referenced stories about Sherlock Holmes and other master detectives, *Go West* was a Western about the life of cowboys in contemporary America and *The Navigator* (1924) was the result of a unique opportunity to charter an ocean liner, the story then being constructed around this vessel. *Our Hospitality* was very loosely based on the infamous nineteenth-century Southern feud between the Hatfields and the McCoys (renamed the Canfields and the McKays in the film), and *The General*, as already mentioned, was based on a book.

Harking back to the central conflict at the heart of his stage work, many of his short films and *The Saphead*, Keaton and his writers fairly consistently developed the feature stories with a particular emphasis on the relationship between the young protagonist and his own father or, more frequently, the father of the girl he loves. The protagonist of *Three Ages* is initially rejected, in two of the three stories, by the girl's father as the less deserving of two suitors (in the modern story, the girl's mother finds him wanting). In *Our Hospitality*, the Keaton character – Willie McKay – falls in love with the daughter of a man who, unbeknownst to him, is involved in a long-running feud with his family and hence tries to kill him. The protagonist of *Sherlock Jr.* (referred to simply as 'a boy' in an intertitle) is tricked by his rival for the girl's affections and ejected from her house by her father (played once again by Joe Keaton), who is led to believe that he is a thief.

The girl's father makes an appearance at the beginning of *The Navigator*, but, for once, does not block her romance with Keaton's character, Rollo Treadway; instead, it is an attack on the father and the ship he owns which helps to bring the two young people together. There are no fathers in *Seven Chances*, but in this film the stipulation in his late grandfather's will that he should be married by his twenty-seventh birthday causes the protagonist Jimmie Shannon to alienate the girl he has been in love with for years. In *Go West*, Keaton plays a hapless would-be cowboy, listed as 'Friendless' in the credits, who initially fails to impress the ranch owner he works for; when, however, he befriends a cow, the owner's daughter takes an interest in him, and her father is willing to sanction their union after Friendless has saved him from ruin. In *Battling Butler*, the Keaton character (Alfred Butler) is temporarily ejected from his home by his father, who wants him to go on a hunting trip; he falls for a girl whose physically imposing father and brother his valet tries to impress by pretending that Alfred is the boxer 'Battling Butler', a pretence Alfred has to keep up, with disastrous consequences. It is therefore not surprising that in *The General*, it is once again the girl's father who creates problems, by misunderstanding why Johnnie fails to enlist, declaring him a disgrace and thus causing his daughter to break up with him.[34]

These and other continuities across Keaton's output suggest that he and his writers were largely in control of selecting and shaping the stories of their films. However, they were dependent on the businessman in charge of Keaton's production company, who had to approve their projects and also sometimes interfered with their selection of stories by buying the rights to stage plays, which he then expected them to adapt.[35] A closer look at this man reveals that Keaton's film career was as much a family affair as his stage career had been (and as the stories of his films continued to be). From the outset, both Comique and Buster Keaton Productions had been controlled by Joseph Schenck, an entertainment entrepreneur with many business interests, among them amusement parks, theatres and film production companies.[36] The latter included a company for his wife, Norma Talmadge, one of the biggest movie stars of the period,[37] and one for her sister Constance. Another sister, Natalie, was employed by Schenck in an administrative role.[38]

Joseph's brother, Nicholas, was, next to founder Marcus Loew, the top executive of Loew's Inc., a theatre chain that moved into film production and distribution by purchasing Metro in 1920. The two brothers tended to be shareholders as well as office holders in each other's companies, and sometimes coordinated their business activities. In 1916–17, Joseph Schenck had been, among other things, the booking manager for Loew's theatre chain, which at that point mainly presented vaudeville acts, among them 'The Three Keatons'. It is quite likely that it was Schenck who, looking for promising comedians to join the film company he had set up with Arbuckle, convinced Keaton to switch from the Shubert revue to Comique in 1917 and appear in its very first production, *The Butcher Boy*. In 1920, Joseph Schenck then arranged for Keaton's first series of two-reelers to be distributed by Metro, and also for his appearance in *The Saphead*, Metro's high-profile adaptation of a classic stage comedy featuring legendary actor William Crane, which would give Keaton a lot of exposure. When Keaton married Natalie Talmadge on 31 May 1921, he joined what, across the decade, developed into arguably the most powerful clan in the American film industry.

By 1924, Loew's Inc. had bought more film companies so as to form MGM, and Joseph Schenck had achieved such a high profile as an entertainment entrepreneuer and film producer that he was asked to become a partner in, and chairman of the board of, United Artists, a film financing and distribution company set up in 1919 by leading movie stars Chaplin, Douglas Fairbanks and Mary Pickford, and the film director D. W. Griffith.[39] As United Artists suffered from a shortage of films, Schenck used his production companies to ensure a greater supply, which is why, after seven features released by Metro/MGM, *The General* was the first film Buster Keaton Productions made for United Artists. In the year of the film's release, Joseph Schenck became the distributor's president, while, following the death of Marcus Loew, Nicholas became the president of Loew's Inc.[40]

Loew's MGM subsidiary exemplified the main path that film production in the United States had taken since the mid-1910s. Studios had numerous stars, writers, directors and other personnel on long-term contracts, their strictly compartmentalised work being organised and supervised by studio executives, with screenplays serving as detailed blueprints for the finished films, thus facilitating the production of dozens of features per year.[41] Comique and Buster Keaton Productions represented a different production model, based on older practices that had been dominant around 1910 and were by now reserved for major stars and directors.[42] Here, a studio employed a comparatively small number of people, who worked in a less compartmentalised, more collaborative fashion with opportunities to develop their story continuously from the writing stage all the way through to the final edit (instead of having to stick to the blueprint of a detailed continuity script describing individual scenes and shots and listing all intertitles). Such a studio produced a small number of films by the same director and/or featuring the same star, with that star and/or director (rather than a studio executive) being in charge of the overall production process.

Comique and Buster Keaton Productions released, on average, one two-reel comedy every two months, and, from 1923, two five-to-eight-reel features per year, one in the spring, the other in the autumn (only 1926 saw the release of one film rather than two).

No script materials appear to have survived, and Keaton's own recollections, as well as those of his collaborators, indicate that stories for the features were developed collaboratively between Keaton and his writers in the form of prose treatments rather than screenplays.[43] Most of the filmic details, including many gags, were worked out on the set or on location, at which point actors and technical personnel were likely to make important contributions. Without always taking proper credit for it,[44] Keaton directed the actors and the action himself, in most cases collaborating with a co-director whose main responsibility was to focus on dramatic rather than comic scenes and/or to supervise the shoot while Keaton was in front of the camera. Keaton also worked closely with his crew on distinctive ways of staging the action for the camera, of positioning and moving the camera, and of editing the resulting shots.[45] None of this is meant to imply that he was solely in charge and responsible for everything happening on screen. Keaton made his films with a trusted team of familiar collaborators, many of whom contributed ideas of their own.

Yet, once again, it has to be emphasised that all of this depended on Schenck's approval. While Arbuckle had owned half of Comique, Keaton did not own any shares in Buster Keaton Productions; the main shareholders were members of the Schenck and Loew families, and Joseph Schenck was the company's president.[46] Keaton's September 1924 employment contract stipulated many obligations and few rights. He offered 'his exclusive services' and agreed to 'promptly and faithfully comply with the reasonable directions, requests, rules and regulations made by the producer' ('producer' here nominally referred to Buster Keaton Productions, but in practice it was Joseph Schenck).[47] Instead of being given the *right* to control all aspects of production, Keaton accepted the *obligation* that, in addition to acting in the company's films, he would 'render such services in connection with directing, cutting, titling and editing of said pictures as may be requested by the producer'.

In return for all this, Keaton was paid $27,000 for each of the six features he made in the next three years (these turned out to be *Seven Chances*, *Go West*, *Battling Butler*, *The General*, *College* [1927] and *Steamboat Bill, Jr.* [1928]), which amounts to a weekly salary of about $1,000, plus 25 per cent of the combined net profits (for Buster Keaton Productions) of all six films.[48] This was a lot of money by the standards of the time (the average *annual* income of employees in the United States in 1924 was $1,200),[49] but only a fraction of the income of Chaplin and Lloyd or other major stars (including Norma Talmadge), who could earn between $10,000 and $30,000 per week.[50] As the next chapter shows, Keaton's income reflected the rather limited success of his feature films at the box office, which in turn had a lot to do with his 'frozen-faced' performance.

2 A Trademark and Profits

The press book for *The General* was designed by United Artists to support exhibitors who had booked the film, offering articles that could be used by local newspapers as well as marketing ideas and an order form for advertisements, posters, lobby display cards and other 'accessories'. The dozens of articles frequently refer to the comedian with phrases evoking his reduced facial expressivity: 'the frozen-faced fun-maker', 'the frozen-faced star', 'the frozen-faced comedy star'. The headline of one article announcing the film's arrival at the local cinema reads: 'Buster Keaton Coming in *The General*: "Frozen-Face" in Civil War Comedy Spectacle'. A series of five-panel comic strips which exhibitors could buy and then offer to their local newspapers is entitled 'Little Frozen Face'. One of the suggestions (presented in an item entitled 'Frozen Face') for promoting the film is a contest to be held at the cinema for people who want to 'rival Buster Keaton's impassivity under any circumstances', with prizes awarded to those 'who can keep a straight face when everyone is trying to make them laugh'.

Keaton's 'frozen face' was a kind of trademark, which distinguished him from other comedians (as well as dramatic actors) and thus helped to foreground the particular qualities of his films. As was emphasised in the press book, these qualities included his extraordinary athleticism, which (according to an article entitled 'Buster Keaton Tumbled to Fame') was based on 'a lifetime of training and constant practice, plus a physique envied by many professional athletes', allowing him to perform 'acrobatic stunts which would land the ordinary mortal in the hospital – or the morgue'. In addition, Keaton's feature films – none more so than *The General* – were characterised by his willingness and ability to stage large-scale (and very expensive) action sequences involving

complex machinery and/or huge numbers of extras. Thus, one of the
model reviews in the film's press book noted:

> Thousands of troops are seen in action and real wood-burning Civil War
> locomotives and trains thunder over the rails. One of the engines in the
> picture crashes through a burning trestle to furnish the greatest thrill ever
> filmed. It is a recorded fact that this scene was made at a cost of $40,000 after
> the crash had [initially] been filmed in miniature at an outlay of $1,000.[51]

The branding of Keaton as the frozen-faced comedian known
for his supremely acrobatic stunts and large-scale action sequences
had started in the early 1920s, soon after his promotion to movie
stardom (with his leading role in *The Saphead* and the release of
short films centring on his performance).[52] Before 1920, Keaton had
done a certain amount of exaggerated smiling, laughing and crying
in Arbuckle's films, and during his early stage career a beaming
smile had been an essential part of his performance.[53] But apart
from a brief smile in *The Saphead*, from 1920 onwards Keaton
avoided pronounced facial expressions in his films, and this became
an important element in their marketing, complemented by an
emphasis on his athleticism and, later, also on the scale of the
action featured in them.

Fatty at Coney Island (1917)

Thus, a humorous article in the *New York Morning Telegraph* from January 1921 noted that a press release from Metro, the distributor of Keaton's short films at the time, was referring to him as 'the agile frozen-faced comedian': 'It's the adjective "frozen-faced" which is disturbing us', because – unlike previous designations such as 'sad-faced' – '"frozen-faced" is likely to jar the nerves of the literal minded natives [of California], who will ask "How did he get a face like that in California?"'[54] In the same year, a review contained in Metro's press book for Keaton's *Hard Luck* stated that he had 'taken full advantage of his long acrobatic training on the vaudeville stage to present some novel and skillful gymnastics' in the film.[55] And Metro's press book for Keaton's first feature, *Three Ages*,[56] foregrounded the spectacular sets of the scenes located in Ancient Rome, as well as the film's large number of extras, in articles entitled 'Keaton's *Three Ages* on Monumental Scale', 'Colosseum Set Largest Ever Made for Pictures' and 'Keaton's *Three Ages* Rivals *Robin Hood* for Magnificence and Sets a Record for Laughs' (*Robin Hood*, a spectacular Douglas Fairbanks vehicle, had been the top-grossing film of 1922 in the United States).[57]

The marketing of Keaton's subsequent features, and also their critical reception, continued to emphasise his reduced facial expressivity and enhanced acrobatics, as well as his staging of large-scale action (which involved, for example, an ocean liner in *The Navigator*, a posse made up of hundreds of female extras in *Seven Chances* and thousands of cattle roaming around a city centre in *Go West*).[58] By the time the press book for *The General* was produced, this branding campaign had been so successful that Keaton was not only extremely widely known but was also ranked by critics as (almost) the equal of Chaplin and Lloyd (who based their screen personas on a tramp costume and round glasses, respectively, while prominently featuring smiles in their performances). Thus, in October 1924, the trade paper *Wid's Weekly* declared that Keaton was 'pretty close to the top of the list among the comedians', while the

New York Sun wrote: 'This young man who never smiles is equaled only by Harold Lloyd and Charlie Chaplin in the ability to make others do so.'[59] The following year, the *New York Herald Tribune* called him 'the third of the cinema's trio of major comedians'.[60]

However, in terms of ticket sales, Keaton was no match for Chaplin and Lloyd. From 1923 to 1926, Lloyd's comedies were consistently among the top-grossing films of their year of release in the United States (*Safety Last* and *Why Worry?* at nos. 4 and 5 in 1923, *Hot Water* and *Girl Shy* jointly at no. 4 in 1924, *The Freshman* at no. 3 in 1925 and *For Heaven's Sake* at no. 4 in 1926), while *The Gold Rush*, the only comedy Chaplin released during these years, was the second biggest hit of 1925.[61] The US rentals for each of these films (that is, the money cinemas paid to the distributor for the right to screen it) amounted to between $1.3 million and $2.7 million.[62] In addition, the strongly comedy-inflected, spectacular adventure films starring Fairbanks, who was known for his on-screen acrobatics (as well as his infectious smile), ranked highly in the annual charts – *The Thief of Bagdad* at no. 3 in 1924, *Don Q, Son of Zorro* at no. 4 in 1925 and *The Black Pirate* at no. 4 in 1926 – with domestic rentals of between $1.5 million and $1.7 million.[63] By contrast, the seven features Keaton released from 1923 to 1926 each only earned between $450,000 and $750,000 in US rentals.[64]

Judging by the many negative comments of critics, Keaton's 'frozen face' was likely to have been an important factor in his limited popularity. This is not to say that there were no positive evaluations of his reduced facial expressivity. The *New York Times*, for example, found that it was a good fit for the story of *Our Hospitality*: 'In a perfectly serious way, in fact a reflection of his expressionless physiognomy, Keaton's comicality begins by introducing two hating families.'[65] In its assessment of *Battling Butler*, the paper noted that, despite the fact that Keaton's 'countenance is as imperturbable as ever', 'information' about his thoughts and feelings could be 'obtained through occasional movements of his eyes and his mouth'.[66] 'His pantomime, as ever, is very eloquent', wrote the *New York Evening Post* in a review of *Go West*, presumably referring to Keaton's ability to express himself through posture and gestures as well as through the very subtle deployment of facial muscles.[67] And reviewing *Battling Butler*, the *New York Telegraph* declared that Keaton 'proves again he is one of the few real masters of the art of pantomime'.[68]

Such comments are, however, in the minority when compared with critical statements like this one about *Go West*: '[There is] a certain wistfulness about that blank mask of the agile and inventive Keaton, but his complete lack of expression does prevent him from being anything of a master of pathos.'[69] Even the film's positive review in the *New York Telegram* noted: 'his art would lose nothing by an occasional relaxation of his facial muscles'.[70] The review of *Battling Butler* in a Hollywood paper stated that more than an hour 'of his painfully expressionless countenance is apt to become excruciatingly tiresome', and the *Los Angeles Express* concluded: 'it is to be feared that his perfectly blank countenance is going to handicap him in time. It deprives him of the great value of mimetics, and makes for a monotonous note all through his comedies.'[71] In its review of *The Navigator*, the *New York World* declared that he was a 'bad ... actor', presumably because, in the paper's opinion, in his physical performances he failed to project a series of individualised, convincing and engaging characters.[72] Thus, many critics felt that Keaton's reduced facial expressivity made it impossible for audiences to perceive and share his characters' emotions, which in turn might cause disengagement from these characters and their stories, leading to boredom – and limited success at the box office.

Whether such limited success would undermine the financial viability of Buster Keaton Productions depended on how much its features cost. The distribution contract between the company and Metro from 28 May 1923 covered three features, with an option for another three releases, and it stipulated that Metro would pay Buster Keaton Productions an advance of $200,000 upon delivery of each film (to be recouped by the distributor from rentals).[73] This was probably the amount Joseph Schenck calculated each film should cost so that delivery of one film generated the funds needed to produce another. In later interviews, Keaton also remembered pre-*General* budgets of just over $200,000.[74]

To determine the profitability of Keaton's features for Buster Keaton Productions, I therefore assume that (with a notable exception to be discussed shortly) each feature before *The General* cost around $200,000.[75] This was above the average budget across the American film industry as a whole,[76] but below the average budget – of $250,000 – of MGM releases (MGM being the company that Metro became part of in 1924, as noted earlier).[77] MGM's releases earned about 30 per cent of their total revenues outside the United States.[78] An appendix to the distribution contract between Buster Keaton Productions and Metro suggests that foreign income for Keaton's films might have been as low as 20 per cent of the total. In the calculations that follow, I assume that the foreign share was 25 per cent of the total.

According to the distribution contract, the rentals Metro/MGM received from exhibitors at home and abroad was divided in the following way with Buster Keaton Productions: the distributor would recoup its advance by initially taking 65 per cent of domestic rentals and 80 per cent of foreign rentals; the remaining 35 per cent and 20 per cent, respectively, also went to the distributor as a fee for its services. In addition to negotiating with exhibitors and delivering film prints to cinemas, Metro/MGM's services included advertising for the films it distributed; the average cost of these services (at MGM about $300,000 per film in the mid-1920s) was higher than the average production budget (of $250,000).[79] Once Metro/MGM had recouped its advance, all further rental income would be split 50/50 between the distributor and Buster Keaton Productions.

The first three releases of Buster Keaton Productions each earned about $500,000 in the United States.[80] From this, $310,000 (all figures are rounded) went to Metro/MGM; 65 per cent of this sum allowed the distributor to recoup its advance, the other 35 per cent was part of its distribution fee.[81] The remaining $190,000 plus foreign income of perhaps around $170,000 would be divided equally between the distributor and Buster Keaton Productions, each receiving $180,000. If the film's budget was indeed covered by Metro/MGM's advance, this $180,000 would have been a profit for Buster Keaton Productions.[82] As *Go West* and *Seven Chances* had domestic rentals of around $600,000, for each of these two films the estimated profit for Buster Keaton Productions was around $250,000. These are very respectable profits. However, cost overruns could easily threaten profitability. In August 1924, *Variety* reported that the final budget of *The Navigator* had gone up to $385,000.[83] Luckily, the film's domestic rentals were $680,000, significantly more than for all but one of the other features made by Buster Keaton Productions before *The General* (the exception being *Battling Butler*, which earned $750,000), so that the company made a profit of $125,000.[84] If, however, domestic rentals had been $500,000 – as was the case for *Three Ages*, *Our Hospitality* and *Sherlock Jr.* – Buster Keaton Productions would have lost money on *The Navigator*.

By the time *The General* was released, then, Keaton had long been recognised as a distinctive and indeed unique comic performer (and film-maker). However, his reduced facial expressivity had been identified as a liability as far as large audience segments were concerned, who, critics reasoned, were likely to object to Keaton irrespective of the film he appeared in, just as others were able to enjoy pretty much all of his work. The *New York Herald Tribune* had stated in a review of *The Navigator*: 'If you like Buster and his methods you like his pictures, otherwise not.'[85] And another critic had admitted that 'unless you are one of those who find him appealing and funny per se I cannot recommend *Go West* as any riot of either mirth or pathos'.[86] This suggested that audience responses to *The General* would be similarly divided between

Keaton's fans and his detractors, with potentially very serious consequences for its performance at the box office. There was therefore a significant financial risk in embarking on the production of an ambitious Civil War movie, which was likely to cost even more than *The Navigator*. So why did Keaton want to do so?

3 The Appeal of Historical Drama

As far as the press book for *The General* was concerned, the film's enormous budget was one of its main selling points,[87] together with Keaton's frozen-faced and acrobatic performance and his direction of large-scale action.[88] Other selling points much written about in the press book were the film's Civil War subject matter (with a particular focus on the presence of huge armies and a battle),[89] its being based on a well-known true story,[90] the historical accuracy of its settings, costumes and props,[91] and its focus on locomotives (including a spectacular crash).[92] All of these selling points were presented in condensed form in an 'advance' article entitled '$500,000 Keaton Comedy Coming to …' (the dots were meant to be replaced with the name of the town in which the exhibitor operated).

The article starts with the statement that 'Buster Keaton's laugh and thrill feature of the Civil War' is '[a]cclaimed as the costliest and most lavish comedy ever produced.' The article then suggests that this comedy in many ways matches, and even surpasses, the great dramas of the day:

it pictures a true story of the sixties, is historically accurate, [and] contains thrills never duplicated in the biggest dramatic photoplays … When critical Hollywood audiences previewed the completed opus they pronounced it not only the greatest comedy they had ever seen, but a feature that ranks in dramatic action with some of the outstanding photoplays of the last decade.

After describing the special efforts made by the production team ('[n]early a year elapsed from the time Buster and his staff began research work on *The General* until the comedy was completed', and location shooting took 'several months'), the article focuses on some of the film's main attractions: 'thousands of National Guardsmen and former soldiers [were] recruited for the battle scenes', and 'three locomotives and scores of cars purchased and converted into wood-burners and equipment of the sixties', one of them being used to film 'the plunge of a speeding locomotive from a burning trestle into a raging river'. The film is said to be 'based on the Andrews railroad raid and locomotive chase, a vivid chapter of the Civil War', and to have been '[p]ersonally directed by the star.'

The press book's understanding of the main selling points of *The General* provides clues to the reasons for Keaton's decision, early in 1926 (around the time he was shooting *Battling Butler*), to embark on such a monumental project. At this point, he must have felt that his star was on the rise, his films, despite minor ups and downs, becoming ever more successful. Whereas Buster Keaton Productions' first three releases – *Three Ages*, *Our Hospitality* and *Sherlock Jr.* – each had domestic rentals of between $450,000 and $540,000, the next three releases – *The Navigator*, *Seven Chances* and *Go West* – each earned between $600,000 and $680,000 (*Battling Butler* was to confirm this upward trend).[93] What is more, as already noted, *The Navigator*'s large budget had translated into the highest earnings of any of his features before 1926, suggesting that it might well be worth investing even more money in the follow-up to *Battling Butler*.

In addition to enjoying increased commercial success, Keaton had been confronted with rising expectations about the quality of the stories his films told. Whereas some critics continued to care mostly about the films' gags and the laughter they elicited, *Life*'s review of *The Navigator*, for example, expressed concern about structural weaknesses, and then predicted: 'Some day Buster Keaton will gain a capability for sustained effort – and then we shall see the funniest comedy in history.'[94] And the *New York Sun* noted that Keaton, Chaplin and Lloyd were pushing each other in the direction of more substantial stories: 'These movie comedians, evidently spurred by intense competition, make it a point to provide a good show', which, in addition to 'their own comic personalities' and 'all the slapstick', involved 'real ideas'.[95]

Keaton and his collaborators were aware of this critical issue and made statements (attributed to Keaton) assuring the public that story qualities were foremost on the comedian's mind. Keaton announced in 1924 that for his next film, *Seven Chances*, he would be 'applying the principles of conventional picture comedy to a story that is good enough to stand on its own merits'; he also talked about combining 'broad' humour with 'subtle satire', so as to appeal to both 'the most critical, discriminating persons', or 'highbrows', and 'the large body of the public': 'Reconciling these two elements is a problem I am bothered with night and day.'[96] The 1924 book *The Truth about the Movies* contained a humorous chapter, published under Keaton's name, about the development of film comedy, which emphasised that present-day comedies were 'bigger and better', relying more on 'comic situations' than isolated gags and also displaying far more lavish production values.[97]

Several critics understood *Go West* very much in these terms (as being more ambitious with regards to story and characterisation

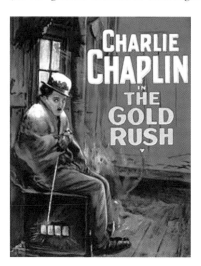

as well as production values) and also detected a more general shift in the output of the major comedians which allowed their films to compete with dramatic productions as far as budgets and emotional appeal were concerned. With reference to *The Gold Rush* (premiered in June 1925) and Lloyd's *The Freshman* (released in September 1925), a *New York Herald Tribune* article about *Go West* from October that year observed:

'The screen comedians are going in for pathos this season. Following the considerable financial returns that have been the reward of Messrs. Chaplin and Lloyd for their most recent efforts, Buster Keaton ... is trying the ways of wistfulness this week.'[98] According to the *New York Telegram*, *Go West* was Keaton's 'biggest picture' yet, exemplifying 'the comedy of today', which involved '[h]undreds of actors and actresses – tons of props – locations hundreds of miles from Hollywood – special trains – thousands of animals – months of activity – staggering costs'; indeed, 'feature length comedies [are now] costing as much or more than the average dramatic production.'[99] The *New York Evening World* thought that the Western dramas which were the main reference point for the comedy of *Go West* were of a much lower quality than Keaton's film: 'The "gag" men of this picture could surely improve the type of picture they have so cleverly satirized.'[100]

This debate about the work of the major comedians encouraged Keaton to think about a truly grandiose project with which he would be able to challenge the biggest dramas on their own terms. His choice of subject matter for this project was probably influenced by the commercial success, in the preceding years, not only of *The Gold Rush* but also of other films about American history, including the epic Westerns *The Covered Wagon* (the second biggest US hit of 1923) and *The Iron Horse* (no. 1 in 1924), as well as *America* (no. 6 in 1924), D. W. Griffith's movie about the War of Independence.[101] These films and others (also set in the distant or more recent past), such as the biblical epic *The Ten Commandments* (no. 2 in 1923), the swashbuckler *The Sea Hawk* (no. 2 in 1924) and especially the World War I drama *The Big Parade* (no. 1 in 1925), suggested that the spectacular staging of large-scale violent conflict had a particular appeal for audiences at the time.

Keaton already had some experience with making historical films. As noted earlier, two of the three stories making up Buster Keaton Productions' first feature, *Three Ages*, are set in the past, and the film's marketing had highlighted the monumental scale of the

Roman episode's sets and cast. The marketing of *Our Hospitality* had emphasised Keaton's serious efforts to recreate the past as a way of distancing this release from the slapstick comedy of his earlier work. Keaton had been quoted as saying: 'I've heard mothers complain from time to time … that their children were getting nothing but buffoonery in comedies. Consequently, I've tried to do something that will be educational, without losing anything in the matter of laughs.'[102] The film had been described as 'an historically accurate picture of life in the United States in 1830', revealing 'seriousness of purpose', and the train featured in it was said to be an 'exact duplicate' of the original.[103] The *New York Times* had called the film's 'mixture' of historical drama and comedy 'extremely pleasing',[104] and *Variety* had declared that its 'novelty melange of dramatics, low comedy, laughs and thrills' turned *Our Hospitality* into 'one of the best comedies ever produced for the screen'.[105] While *Go West*, released in November 1925, tells a story set in the present, it portrays a way of life closely associated with nineteenth-century America.

Therefore, it is not surprising that when, at the beginning of 1926, Keaton looked for a subject for his grandest production yet, American history of the previous century was at the forefront of his mind – and also trains. Trains had already featured more or less prominently in many of his previous short films and features (for example, in *Our Hospitality*, *Sherlock Jr.* and *Go West*). Indeed, the train journey in *Our Hospitality* had attracted a lot of attention, with *Variety* predicting that it 'will go down in screen annals as a comedy classic'.[106] What is more – next to *The Gold Rush* – the biggest hit about nineteenth-century America of the preceding two years had been *The Iron Horse*, a film about building the first transcontinental railroad in the 1860s. Intriguingly, the film's opening sequences feature Abraham Lincoln and reference the Civil War, in particular the occasion, in 1862, when Lincoln signs an Act of Congress facilitating the railroad project, and thus rejects the arguments of those who do not want to divert any resources from

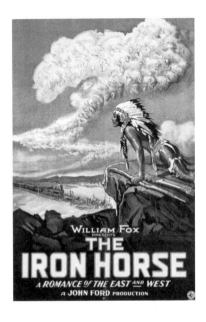

the Union's battle against the Confederacy. The film also highlights the fact that after the end of the Civil War, the former enemies work together on this great project.

Then, in January 1926, *Hands Up!*, a film starring Raymond Griffith, a popular comedian from the second rank behind Chaplin, Lloyd and Keaton, received good reviews.[107] The film is set during the Civil War and features a Southern spy who tries to prevent a shipment of gold from a Nevada mine back to the East. The story, which for long stretches has more of a Western feel (due to the presence of stagecoaches, Native Americans, etc.), is peacefully resolved when the Civil War ends, allowing the hero to prepare for a wedding with both daughters of the mine owner (made possible by his departure to polygamous Salt Lake City).[108]

The positive critical reception of *Hands Up!*, together with the huge success of *The Iron Horse* and other recent films about nineteenth-century America, as well as Keaton's earlier, quite positive experiences with portraying the American way of life in the previous century and his particular fascination with staging action on trains – all of these help to explain why he came to settle on the Civil War and more particularly on 'the Andrews railroad raid and locomotive chase' (in the words of the press book) as the subject of his most ambitious project yet, a project which would, he hoped, allow him to compete not only with other comedians but also with the great dramas of the day.

Late in 1925 or early in 1926, Clyde Bruckman suggested a book about the Andrews raid by William Pittenger to Keaton (more about this volume later).[109] Bruckman, who had co-written the first five features of Buster Keaton Productions and had then been employed as a writer on Lloyd's two biggest hits (*The Freshman* and *For Heaven's Sake*),[110] would not only work as a writer on *The General* but also become Keaton's co-director on this film (the credits read 'Written and Directed by Buster Keaton and Clyde Bruckman'). In later years, he was remarkably modest about his contributions to Keaton's films: 'Buster was his own best gagman. ... You seldom saw his name in the story credits. But I can tell you ... that those wonderful stories were ninety percent Buster's. ... Most of the direction was his [as well].'[111] Marion Mack, who played Annabelle, also remembered that 'Buster directed most of the scenes', which did not, however, involve much guidance for her performance: 'I sort of directed myself. I mean, they tell you your scene, but none of the directors hardly ever act it for you.'[112] According to Mack, there was no 'regular shooting script', only an 'outline'; every evening during the shoot, Keaton and his writers would get together 'to talk over the gags' and to make 'notes ... of what they were going to do': 'Buster was really good on thinking up these gags'.[113] On the set and on location, the actors and the crew were encouraged to come up with new 'bits of business': 'if anybody had an idea they would try it and see how it played'.[114]

When first contemplating an adaptation of Pittenger's book, Keaton was shooting (in January and February 1926) and previewing *Battling Butler* (in March).[115] Normally, this film would have been released soon afterwards as a follow-up to the autumn 1925 release of *Go West*, but for unknown reasons it only came out in August. Possibly Keaton and his team became so absorbed in preparations for their Civil War movie that there was a delay in putting the final touches (in response to the preview) to *Battling Butler*. In addition to developing the story for *The General*, preparations for the shoot included extensive historical research,

the procurement of props and costumes, location scouting and
the building of large sets on location and at the Keaton studio in
Hollywood (as well as the purchase and reconstruction of several
locomotives and numerous train cars). A press book article entitled
'Keaton Worked Six Months before Filming One Scene' put it
as follows:

Technical and research workers traveled thousands of miles ... in their quest
for data in connection with the Civil War story. Thousands of uniforms had to
be specially tailored, great quantities of old rifles, pistols, swords, artillery
pieces and other relics assembled and tons of properties and acres of sets built.

At the story's original locations in Georgia and Tennessee,
Keaton encountered various problems: he felt that the scenery
would not work for what he had in mind, and there were also local
objections to a comedy being made about this Civil War episode.[116]
So Keaton's location scouts found a suitable place in Oregon, and at
the end of May 1926 he moved a production team of sixty people
and many train-car loads of equipment to the small town of Cottage
Grove. Once the Marietta set had been constructed there, filming
started on 8 June. Shooting – on this and other sets, as well as on
various locations in and around Cottage Grove – continued until
the end of July, when forest fires disrupted proceedings. Even after
they had been brought under control, smoke clouds made it difficult
to continue. So on 6 August, Keaton went back to Hollywood to
film interiors at his studio. The production company returned to
Oregon on 29 August, where the location shoot wrapped on
18 September. This was followed by another week of shooting at
the Keaton studio. Keaton and his editors then worked in a cutting
room he had installed in his house in Beverly Hills.

Together with the forest fires (as well as some minor
accidents), Keaton's production method, which privileged flexibility
and spontaneity over detailed pre-planning, prolonged the shoot
and thus drove up the cost, as did the great scope of the film's story

and the desire for grand spectacle (most notably in the scene in which the Texas crashes down with the collapsing bridge). So it is not surprising that the film's final budget was $415,000,[117] which was less than the $500,000 proudly announced in the press book, yet still about twice as much as any previous feature release by Buster Keaton Productions (with the exception of *The Navigator*). The pursuit of historical accuracy in terms of settings, costumes and props was an important cost factor as well, yet, as we will see in the next chapter, it did not apply to the construction of the story, which took some liberties with historical fact.

4 From Book to Film

In an article entitled 'Keaton Film Based on Historical Fact', the press book for *The General* explained the film's 'authentic Civil War background':

Andrews and a score of Union men captured the locomotive, 'The General', at Big Shanty, Georgia, in April, 1862, hoping to make their way to Chattanooga, burning bridges and destroying the [rail]road on their way, thus preventing the Southern army from succoring Chattanooga. The success of this raid might have turned the tide of the war.

Another article – 'Historical Accuracy in Keaton Picture' – explained:

The pages of one history book mention a young engineer who chased the whole lot of them, both as a duty to the South and to rescue his iron friend and companion, 'The General'. This engineer comes out of history's pages in the frozen-faced guise of Buster Keaton.

The book referred to here is Reverend William Pittenger's *Capturing a Locomotive: A History of Secret Service in the Late War*, which had originally been published in 1885.[118]

As a young man, Pittenger had been a member of J. J. Andrews's team, and he assures the reader that 'all fictitious embellishments have been rejected' and '[n]o pains have been spared to ascertain the exact truth.'[119] The book's story is told in twenty-one chapters, taking up 332 pages (in addition, there are fourteen pages of appendices and eight pages of preliminary materials). The first three chapters introduce some of the personnel, and deal with the raiders' preparations in a Union camp in Tennessee, as well as their infiltration into Georgia. Pittenger explains that the main objective of the raid was to capture a Confederate train in Big Shanty, Georgia, and then to move north towards Chattanooga, Tennessee, burning bridges along the way, so that the Confederates would find it difficult to support Chattanooga against an imminent attack by the Union army.[120] He reveals that, at the time, he believed that the successful execution of this plan might help to bring the war to an early end.[121]

Chapters 4–6 relate how the spies boarded a train in Marietta, Georgia, and captured the locomotive (which was indeed called 'General') during the breakfast break in Big Shanty on 12 April 1862. They then raced back towards Northern lines, but, due to a number of unforeseen problems, were unable to burn any bridges and eventually decided to abandon their train a few miles south of Chattanooga (the last town on the line still in Southern hands) and escaped on foot into the woods. Chapters 7–9 deal with the desperate flight of the raiders and their eventual capture. The rest of the story (Chapters 10–21, taking up 171 pages – that is more than half of the total) deals with the incarceration of the raiders in several prisons, their trials, the execution of eight prisoners (including Andrews) in June 1862, various attempts at escape (during one of which eight of them got away in October 1862) and, finally, the exchange and return home of the remaining six prisoners (including Pittenger) in March 1863.

A self-declared abolitionist,[122] Pittenger foregrounds slavery as a decisive issue early on in his story, mentioning the Southern 'enthusiasm in behalf of the cause of disunion and slavery' and also his horror and disgust, upon first entering Georgia, at hearing 'a slave-holder talk of hunting negroes with blood-hounds'.[123] Later on, when describing his attempt to get from the abandoned General back to Union lines, he notes that, for Southerners, '[t]he dark institution of slavery rendered the work of hunting down fugitive men very familiar.'[124] During his flight, he received help from a 'negro, who, like all of his color, was ready to do anything for fugitives, with whom he had a fellow-feeling';[125] helpful African Americans also appear later in the story.[126] When describing the horrendous conditions which he and some of his comrades experienced in the Chattanooga prison, he holds '[t]he system of slavery ... primarily responsible', because such prisons were designed to punish slaves.[127] This leads him to contemplate the terrible suffering of slaves, and to pose a rhetorical question: 'Can we too often thank God that the whole awful system of slavery has been swept away?' (swept away, that is, by the Confederacy's defeat in the Civil War).[128] Throughout the book, Pittenger highlights the extreme and all-pervasive brutality of Southern society, concluding that 'the natural result of slavery' is 'making men barbarous and inhuman even to whites'.[129]

Keaton and his writers made no use of the material relating to the plight of slaves and the general impact of slavery, but nor did their version of the story feature the happy and loyal slaves of so many other Civil War films of the period.[130] In *Hands Up!*, for example, Raymond Griffith's Southern spy meets an African American man in Nevada. They know each other from the South, which means that this man is a former slave – and yet he is very pleased when he recognises the spy and eager to help him with his mission against the Union. By contrast, the only African Americans in *The General* appear at the beginning, carrying the luggage of the passengers disembarking from Johnnie's train; they are not portrayed as loyal servants, nor are they shown to be particularly happy. Since Keaton and his writers reworked the story so that the raiders were able to make it all the way back to their own lines, the film fails to reproduce the book's criticism of their inhuman treatment in Southern prisons. However, it does, I will argue, offer a critical perspective on Southern 'enthusiasm' for war.

Apart from a brief early scene explaining the objectives of the raid, the film does not deal with its preparatory stage, and instead focuses almost exclusively on material from Chapters 4–6.

Having boarded the train in Marietta, the raiders uncoupled the passenger cars during a break in Big Shanty, because, Pittenger explains, they 'would only have been an incumbrance', and then sped off.[131] They cut the telegraph wire, damaged the track by removing rails, placed obstacles on it, loaded fresh supplies of wood and water, and then continued obstructing the track 'by breaking open the hind end of the last box-car, and shoving [its contents] out one by one'[132] – all of which is also shown in a streamlined fashion in the film, often reproducing the action described in the book (such as the one in the last quotation) very closely (see p. 48). There were numerous complications holding up the stolen train's journey towards Chattanooga (to do, among other things, with trains running on the same track in the opposite direction, as well as the suspicions of people in the towns the raiders passed through) which did not make it into the film. But the most surprising of these complications became the very foundation of its story.

Pittenger states that he was able to reconstruct the 'strange' events that had unfolded '[f]rom printed accounts published contemporaneously by several of those engaged in the pursuit, as well as from personal responses to inquiries made regarding the most material points'.[133] When the raiders made off with the stolen train in Big Shanty, the engineer William A. Fuller shouted 'Come on!' to his assistant Jefferson Cain and to Anthony Murphy, 'manager of the State railroad shops at Atlanta', and 'started at a full run after the flying train', followed by the other two, yet being 'greeted with loud laughter and ironical cheers by the excited multitude' of bystanders: 'To all appearances it was a foolish and hopeless chase.'[134] Fuller believed that the train had been captured by deserters who

would use his engine only to get a mile or two beyond the guard line [of the nearby Confederate army camp], and then abandon it. He was therefore anxious to follow closely in order to find the engine and return it for his passengers at the earliest moment possible.[135]

In the film, it is only Johnnie who pursues the stolen train.
He shares Fuller's initial assumption about the identity of the
thieves; a dialogue intertitle reads: 'Three men stole my General.
I think they are deserters.'

Back to the book: After running for two miles, the three
pursuers met 'a party of workmen with a hand-car ..., and these
most welcome reinforcements were at once pressed into the
service'.[136] However, when the handcar hit the spot where the
raiders had removed some of the rails, the pursuers crashed and
suddenly 'found themselves floundering in a ditch half filled with
water, and their hand-car imbedded in the mud beside them'.[137]
Having also noticed the severed telegraph wire, by this time Fuller
and the others were quite sure that they were not dealing with
deserters who would soon abandon the train. After lifting the
handcar back on the track, they continued their pursuit and reached
Etowah station, where they commandeered a train (the 'Yonah'),
which, after encountering various obstacles, they had to replace

with another train, the 'Shorter', and finally with the 'Texas'; this last train was loaded with volunteers eager to fight the thieves. When the Texas was confronted by further obstructions on the rail, 'Fuller, who had stationed himself for that purpose on the end of the tender which ran ahead, would jump off' and remove them.[138]

Once again, the film simplifies the action, but reproduces many details. Johnnie's handcar lands in a stream. At the station he reaches afterwards, he commandeers a train, along with dozens of soldiers, but, upon its departure, it turns out that the car with the soldiers was uncoupled and is therefore left behind. Later on, Johnnie runs ahead of the train to remove obstacles but gets awkwardly caught on its cow-catcher.

When, in the book, the Texas finally came within sight of the General, the raiders were shocked: '[The pursuers'] train was in plain sight. We could even see that they were well armed. There seemed to be no resource but flight.'[139] In order to block the Texas, they uncoupled their 'hindmost car', but then observed that 'Fuller saw the car we dropped, and by promptly having his engine reversed, reduced the collision to merely a smart shock', coupled the rogue car to the engine and then moved forward again with 'scarcely diminished' speed; this sequence of events was repeated with a second car.[140] After crossing several bridges (which, because of their pursuit by the Texas, they had no time to set fire to), and passing through various towns, the raiders eventually managed to leave a burning car behind in 'a long covered bridge', only to see 'the enemy pushing our blazing car before them over the bridge' and then 'to the first side track, which happened not to be far away'.[141] Again, while simplifying the action, the film used many of the book's details, such as the incident on the covered bridge and the use of a side track to get rid of the burning car.[142]

Towards the end of Chapter 6, the book's narrative goes in a direction which the film does not follow. The raiders knew that there were two train lines leaving the town of Dalton, which they had just passed through. The one they were on would take them directly to Chattanooga, but the other could also be used to get there, albeit in a roundabout fashion. Since telegraph lines ran alongside railways, Fuller would be able to send a message about the capture of the General to Chattanooga via the second line, giving the Confederate army stationed there time to prepare for the raiders' arrival. Faced with this situation, Andrews ordered his team to abandon the train before it reached Chattanooga and to scatter into the woods.

In Chapter 7, entitled 'A Night in the Woods', Pittenger describes his first night on the run, remarking on the 'drenching rain' and the fact that he 'knew nothing of the locality in which I found myself': 'It was more like trying to run away from danger in a nightmare than any waking sensation.'[143] Keaton and his writers incorporated aspects of this chapter into Johnnie's story. He abandons his train in enemy territory, escapes into the woods and gets soaked by torrential rain during the night. According to an intertitle, Johnnie is 'hopelessly lost' when he stumbles on the Union headquarters. After learning about the enemy's plans and liberating Annabelle, he returns to the forest, where he and Annabelle endure nightmarish experiences, involving lightning strikes, a bear and a bear trap.

The remainder of the film also utilises two ideas from Chapter 6. Pittenger reports that it might have been possible for the raiders to attack their pursuers while they were clearing the tracks, to capture their train and reverse it so that it would collide 'with the next pursuing train' (Fuller had made sure that reinforcements were sent after the Texas).[144] During their escape on the General, Johnnie and Annabelle are pursued by the Texas, which in turn is followed by a supply train; on two occasions, Johnnie manages to orchestrate a collision between the two. Finally, the film picks up on Pittenger's praise of Fuller, in particular 'his energy, skill, and daring' and the fact that he single-handedly saved the day: 'All the evidence goes to show that the Confederacy had no other available man who could have saved the bridges on the Western and Atlantic Railroad that day.'[145] Not only did the legislature of Georgia give him 'a vote of thanks for his brilliant services', but '[t]he Confederate authorities [also] gave him the rank of captain'.[146] At the end of *The General*, Johnnie is made a lieutenant.

With few exceptions, then, the film draws only on the fifty-five pages of Chapters 4–6 (that is 17 per cent of the total, if preliminary materials and appendices are excluded). And the vast majority of the material taken from the book was incorporated into the part of the film which starts with the scene showing how Andrews and Thatcher map out the raid and ends with Johnnie abandoning the Texas; this part lasts just under 21 minutes (when played at 25 frames per second [fps]),[147] – that is, 28 per cent of the film's length (if its credits and 'The End' title are excluded).

It is reasonable to assume that, when encountering Pittenger's book, Keaton and his writers first identified Chapters 4–6 as the core for a film story, and then added an introductory section as well as new material to develop and conclude the narrative. Keaton and his writers had taken a similar approach to the writing of *The Navigator*, which Keaton often declared to have been his favourite among his own movies apart from *The General*.[148] As mentioned earlier, that project got started when an ocean liner became available quite cheaply for charter.[149] The decision was made that action set on the liner would in effect constitute the (very long) middle of the film and revolve around the Keaton protagonist and a young woman, the two being alone on the ship and completely out of their depths (as well as being initially unaware of each other's presence). The next step was to write the film's opening, which would explain who these two characters were and how they ended up alone on an ocean liner. Also needed was an ending that would bring them back to civilisation (this turned out to be very short).

When looking at Chapters 4–6 of Pittenger's book, Keaton and his writers seem to have decided very quickly that their story would focus on Fuller rather than the raiders. This was in line with Civil War movies of the time (such as *The Birth of a Nation* and

Hands Up!), which often took the side of the Confederacy.[150]
What is more, as in all of Keaton's features – and indeed as in most
Hollywood movies[151] – the action storyline of the chase would have
to be complemented with a romantic storyline. The ingenious
solution was to place the girl on the stolen train (she is the only
passenger returning to it during the break in the journey). At this
point, it was conceivable that the film would simply tell the story
of how the Keaton protagonist (a character based on Fuller, the
other pursuers being removed so as to focus all attention on the
star) single-handedly foils the Union plot and wins the heart of the
abducted female passenger in the process.

However, Keaton and his writers opted for a more expansive
story, which had an introductory section (similar to that of *The
Navigator*) dealing with the relationship between the protagonist
and the girl before they embark on their fateful journey, and also
ended his pursuit of the General with him leaving his train in
Union territory, not with the raiders abandoning theirs in Confederate
territory. This then allowed the protagonist to liberate the girl from
captivity and steal back the General. Presumably because it was felt
that any ambitious Civil War film had to have a major military
confrontation and, as previously mentioned, such confrontations
were popular with cinema audiences, Keaton and his writers moved
one of the battles involving the advancing Union army – which,
according to the book, took place far away from the locations of
the locomotive chase – to the territory across which the protagonist
escapes on the General. Let's take a closer look, then, at how the
film is structured.

5 A Film in Six Parts

Despite the fact that the capture of the General by Andrews's raiders and
Fuller's pursuit of the stolen train took place in Georgia, *The General*'s
press book placed a lot of emphasis on Chattanooga, Tennessee. Not only
do many of its articles point out that the raiders intended to take their
train all the way to Chattanooga but they also refer to the 'railroad raid
and locomotive chase in Tennessee and Georgia' as if the raiders' train
had indeed reached Chattanooga.[152] One review states that in the
film, 'a band of Northerners steal "The General" and dash through
Tennessee and Georgia with the wood-burning locomotive'.[153]
An article attributed to Keaton notes that '[i]t was our original plan to
film the picture in Tennessee, the locale of the chief part of the story' –
when, in fact, only the preparations for the raid took place there.[154]

In later writings about *The General*, the film has continued
to be associated with Chattanooga. For example, despite all the
detective work John Bengtson carried out to match the film's diegetic
locations to the locations in Oregon where *The General* was shot, he
nevertheless makes the mistake of identifying the town in which the
story ends as Chattanooga.[155] While this chapter is mostly concerned
with the structure of *The General*, I also want to pay attention to the
film's geography, because, although deceptively simple at first sight
(after all, most of the action takes place along a single railway line),
it is in fact quite confusing and easily misunderstood.

The story of *The General* can be divided into six parts,
together lasting (when shown at 25 fps) 74 minutes and 34 seconds,
excluding 48 seconds of opening credits and 5 seconds of 'The End'.
The first part, which I propose to call 'Rejection', is set in Marietta
on 12 April 1861, the day the Confederate army attacks Fort
Sumter and thus starts the Civil War. Annabelle's brother brings the

news that 'Fort Sumter has been fired upon', to which her father replies: 'Then the war is here.' Johnnie is rejected by the recruiting officer and then by Annabelle's father and brother, as well as by Annabelle herself. This part is 10 minutes and 10 seconds long.

Part 2 – 'Loss and Pursuit' – is set a year later in a Union army camp 'North of Chattanooga', and also on the train line from Marietta to Chattanooga. It deals with the planning of the raid, Annabelle's boarding of Johnnie's train in Marietta, the theft of the General and Annabelle's abduction in Big Shanty and Johnnie's pursuit, which includes his commandeering of the Texas in Kingston (the town's name being visible in some of the shots). This part ends with his abandonment of the engine and retreat into the forest. It lasts 20 minutes and 57 seconds. Apart from the opening scene in the Union army camp, we can assume that it takes place on 12 April 1862 (the date of the historical raid). But where does Johnnie's journey end? The map shown in the first scene of Part 2 has the train

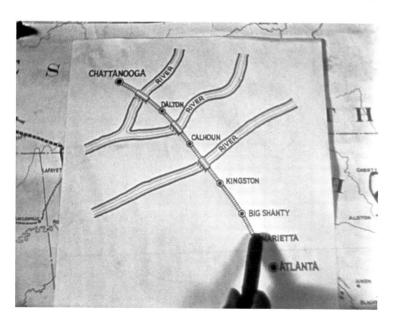

line terminating in Chattanooga, which means that Johnnie abandons the Texas *before* he reaches that town. It is also important to note that shortly before the scene in which he retreats into the forest, an intertitle explains that '[t]he Southern army facing Chattanooga is ordered to retreat'; the Confederate army is then shown to turn around, moving in the opposite direction from the one in which the Texas is travelling (and being pursued by the advancing 'victorious Northern army').[156] This suggests that Johnnie's escape happens somewhere in the (southeastern) vicinity of Chattanooga.

The third part – 'Reversal' – takes place during the night of 12–13 April 1862. By accident, Johnnie finds the Union headquarters, which one might initially assume to be located near the camp shown at the beginning of Part 2 – that is, north of Chattanooga – unless, of course, the Union army's advance has, in the meantime, moved headquarters further south, which would make it more likely that Johnnie can reach them on foot. In any case, he learns about the enemy's plans and liberates Annabelle, before going back into the forest. This part lasts 8 minutes and 45 seconds.

In the fourth part – 'Retrieval and Escape' – which takes place the following morning (13 April 1862), Johnnie and Annabelle find themselves next to a huge army camp and railway depot, presumably on the outskirts of Chattanooga, from where the train line runs to Dalton, Calhoun, Kingston, Big Shanty and Marietta (see the map again). Johnnie and Annabelle recapture the General and escape on it. But which of the three bridges on the map is the Rock River bridge that they set fire to? One would assume that it is the very first one they reach (between Chattanooga and Dalton), because they would want to delay their pursuers and the supply train's advance as soon as possible. This means that the town the General is heading for afterwards is Dalton.

Although there is no clear marker of the end of Part 4 (all the others end with a fade-out followed by an intertitle), I propose to regard the last shot before the General's arrival in Dalton as the end of Part 4. On that basis, Part 4 is 20 minutes and 35 seconds long. Part 5 – 'Warning and Battle' – takes place (also on 13 April 1862) in Dalton and at the Rock River bridge. In town, Johnnie informs the Confederate general about the Union plan, and then joins, and helps to win, the battle at the bridge. This part lasts 9 minutes and 5 seconds. The film's final part – 'Reward' – takes place a little bit later on the same day back in Dalton, where Johnnie is finally enlisted, while also sealing his romantic relationship with Annabelle. It is 5 minutes and 2 seconds long.

Here, then, is a schematic breakdown of the film:[157]

0:00 Credits

0:48 Part 1:   *Rejection* (10 min. 10 sec.)
                Daytime, 12 April 1861:
                Marietta, Georgia

10:58 Part 2:   *Loss and Pursuit* (20 min. 57 sec.)
                a) Night-time, early April 1862 (1 min. 37 sec.):
                Union camp north of Chattanooga
                b) Daytime, 12 April 1862 (19 min. 20 sec.):
                Railroad from Marietta via Big Shanty and
                Kingston to near Chattanooga, Tennessee

31:55 Part 3:   *Reversal* (8 min. 45 sec.)
                Night-time, 12–13 April 1862:
                Forest and Union headquarters near Chattanooga

40:40 Part 4:   *Retrieval and Escape* (20 min. 35 sec.)
                Daytime, 13 April 1862:
                Railroad from a depot near Chattanooga via the
                Rock River bridge to near Dalton, Georgia

61:15 Part 5:   *Warning and Battle* (9 min. 5 sec.)
                Daytime, 13 April 1862:
                Dalton and the area around the Rock River bridge

70:20 Part 6:   *Reward* (5 min. 2 sec.)
                Daytime, 13 April 1862:
                Dalton

75:22 'The End'

75:27

The first thing to note is that Parts 2 and 4 mirror each other in many ways, insofar as they are almost exactly the same length and are both mainly concerned with the theft of the General and its pursuit. At 41 minutes and 32 seconds, these two chase-focused parts make up 56 per cent of the film's total. Several actions of the thieves are repeated across these two parts (with important variations in their order and in the details of their execution): uncoupling the majority of the train's cars before the engine is taken; cutting the telegraph wire; changing uniforms; loading wood and filling the water tank; inadvertently dousing the pursuers with water; uncoupling the last car so that it gets in the way of the pursuing train; dropping stuff out of the last remaining car onto the rails; throwing switches so that the pursuing train moves onto a side track; removing Annabelle from the car in which she begins the journey; trying to set fire to a bridge.

However, in the light of the emphasis placed on this repetition in the Keaton literature,[158] it is important to remember that the majority of the actions of both the pursuers and the pursued are *not* repeated, including, from Part 2: Johnnie chasing the General on foot, then on a handcar and a bicycle; the removal of rails by the raiders and the subsequent derailing of Johnnie's handcar; his attempt to gather support (at Kingston); his use of a cannon; his trouble getting rid of the first uncoupled car he encounters; his belated realisation that the front line has moved and he is now in enemy territory; the raiders bombarding him with planks from above (as he goes under the huge bridge they are standing on). Similarly, most of the action in Part 4 is not a repeat of what happened in Part 2, especially the interaction between Johnnie and Annabelle.

There is some repetition with variations between Parts 1, 5 and 6. The first part begins with Johnnie arriving in Marietta in the General's cab, and at the beginning of Part 5 he enters Dalton in the same way, whereas Part 6 starts with him *marching* with the victorious Confederate army into Dalton, and, upon arrival, making a beeline for the General's cab. In Part 1, Johnnie tries unsuccessfully to enlist in the

Confederate army, whereas in Part 5 he joins its battle in a borrowed uniform, and in Part 6 is finally given his own uniform and enlisted. In Part 1, Annabelle's father (together with her brother) sees Johnnie walking away from the recruitment office, and thinks that he has refused to enlist; while in Part 5, her father (soon joined by Annabelle) sits opposite the place where Johnnie (wearing his borrowed uniform) reports to the Confederate general; and, in the final part, the father (together with Annabelle) excitedly observes Johnnie receiving a lieutenant's uniform and being enlisted. Finally, Part 1 concludes with Johnnie sitting on the drive rod of the General, which then starts moving, and Part 6 ends with him in very much the same position – but now joined by Annabelle and without the engine moving.

Parts 1 and 6 have something else in common – namely, that the film's story would make perfect sense without them. Parts 2–5 tell a coherent and complete story about a Southern locomotive engineer becoming a Civil War hero and gaining a female admirer along the way. This shortened version of the film would begin in the Union camp with Thatcher and Anderson explaining their plan for the raid, and end with the defeat of the Union army at the Rock River bridge, Johnnie proudly holding up the Confederate flag before, in a final comic twist, it is revealed that he is not standing on a rock but on the back of a Confederate officer who, when getting up, knocks Johnnie over.

The fact that this was a possible version of the film Keaton and his collaborators *could* have made alerts us to the central importance of Parts 1 and 6 for the film they *wanted* to make. This importance revolves around the strong attachments that Johnnie has from the outset to his engine and to Annabelle, and the ways in which the Civil War interferes with these attachments. Thus, Part 1 focuses centrally on the relationship between Johnnie and Annabelle as well as on his relationship with the General, as the former is disrupted when the Civil War raises the expectation that Johnnie should enlist, which (as we have seen) he is unable to do precisely because his close relationship with the General makes him more valuable to the South as an engineer. As a consequence of this, there is no interaction between Johnnie and Annabelle in Part 2, except for their exchange of looks in the Marietta scene at the beginning of Part 2b. What is more, the Civil War, now interfering with Johnnie's life through the Union raid, also separates him from the General for all of Part 2b, except for the initial scene in Marietta.

In Part 3, Johnnie accidentally sees Annabelle again and the couple is reunited when he rescues her. Also very much by coincidence, at the beginning of Part 4 Johnnie finds the General, and by stealing the engine back (with Annabelle's help), the second important relationship in his life is re-established. The rest of Part 4 then focuses, like Part 1, on his interaction both with the General and with Annabelle. Yet, the Civil War interferes with Johnnie's two relationships once more in Part 5. Upon their arrival in Dalton, he is separated from the General and from Annabelle, and instead of going back to them after reporting to the Southern general, he joins the battle at the Rock River bridge.

At this point, it is worth considering the logic of Annabelle's story across the first five parts. In Part 1, she is initially perfectly at ease with Johnnie courting her, placing the framed picture he gives her in a prominent position in her house. She then disrupts the courtship's expected progression towards marriage by suggesting to him, after her brother and father have departed for the recruitment office, that he should enlist as well. When she is later told by her brother that '[h]e didn't even get in line' and is to be condemned for this failure, she confronts Johnnie next to the General: 'Why didn't you enlist?' His answer is: 'They wouldn't take me.' She accuses him of lying, announces that she will only speak to him again when he wears a uniform and walks off.

So, it is not the outbreak of Civil War on its own but Annabelle's demand that Johnnie should fight, together with her lack of trust in him, which ends their relationship. Annabelle's attitude is informed by the behaviour, expectations and judgments of her brother and father, who in turn represent a male-dominated society that is eager to embark on war. At the beginning of Part 2b (one year of not speaking to Johnnie later), Annabelle goes so far as to taunt him by fondling the medal pinned to her injured brother's uniform (see p. 62). As the medal has presumably been awarded because of the wounds he sustained, Annabelle is in effect trying to shame Johnnie for his lack of injuries, which demonstrates how much her militaristic understanding of a man's patriotic duty has transformed her romantic feelings.

Is it too far-fetched to say that from then on the story is constructed in such a way that Annabelle is being punished for her behaviour towards Johnnie? Reviewers certainly noticed and commented upon how roughly Annabelle – and thus the actress playing her – was treated: '[Mack] is not called upon for any histrionic display but she deserves a medal for surviving the manhandling she receives'; '[s]eldom have we seen a lady so roughly handled'; '[Mack] takes a good portion of punishment in the execution of her part without any apparent ill effects'.[159]

So, here is what happens to Annabelle. Soon after taunting Johnnie, she is abducted and bound by the Union spies; later on, they rudely manhandle her when moving her around. Also, the train she is on is almost hit by a cannon ball. In Part 3, she is imprisoned in a bedroom without any prospect of release in the foreseeable future, and in despair collapses on the bed. When Johnnie, having donned the uniform of a Union guard he has knocked out, creeps into her room, she is understandably alarmed; he has to grab her forcefully, pressing his hand on her mouth to stifle her screams. He then takes her from the confinement – and relative safety – of the room into the forest, where she is soaked by rain and almost hit by lightning, becomes temporarily separated from Johnnie, confronts a bear and is painfully caught in a trap (see p. 63). Despite all this, she is grateful to Johnnie: 'It was so brave of you to risk your life, coming into enemy's country, just to save me.' It is somewhat ironic that she understands his behaviour in romantic terms, never considering the possibility that he may have other (professional or

military) reasons for being in enemy territory. It would appear that, in her mind, romance trumps militaristic patriotism after all. Johnnie is, of course, very happy to accept her interpretation of his actions.

Although Annabelle is now talking to Johnnie again and their courtship seems to be back on track, her 'punishment' is not over yet. In Part 4, she suffers countless indignities. Johnnie stuffs her into a sack, which he then carries to, and deposits in, a boxcar shortly before Union soldiers throw various heavy items on top of her. After his recapture of the General, he looks for her in the boxcar and carelessly tramples all over the sack she is in. When trying to refill the water tank, Annabelle is twice hit by a powerful stream of water. In Part 5, helping Johnnie in his dealings with the Confederate general, she is almost run over by the cavalry and the horse-drawn carts setting off for the Rock River bridge. She only reaches safety when she rejoins her father, leaving Johnnie behind, and being left behind by him in turn, because he runs off to join the battle, thus responding to her earlier demand that he should enlist and fight. In Part 6, except for a brief early scene in which he finds the Union commander in the General's cab, Johnnie continues to be separated from his engine and his girl, but after she and her father have seen him being enlisted, the couple gets together for the concluding moments of the film, which find them sitting on his engine and kissing. Johnnie is finally reunited with his two loves, and all seems well. But is it?

6 Love and War

In order to determine whether the ending of *The General* is as happy as it seems, it is necessary to understand what it is the protagonist sets out to achieve and what he really wants in, and from, life. The film's press book included some surprising answers to these questions. For example, an article entitled 'What It's All About' contains a kind of plot summary which includes material that has little, if any, connection to what is shown in the film. The article begins with the following, quite baffling, statement:

In 1862 there were thousands of patriots, both northerners and southerners, who chafed under the tasks imposed upon them by their respective governments. Many of them, yearning for glory in the first line of fighting, were doomed to serve in less heroic capacities.

The film's protagonist is then introduced as '[o]ne of these unsung heroes', who 'repeatedly tried to enlist in the Confederate army'. He knew that he had been refused because 'the military chieftains decreed' that 'he was of more value to the cause as the engineer of "The General"'. Both 'his friends' and 'his sweetheart' believed that 'he was a slacker', and after the latter 'rejected' him, 'he turned to his only friend, "The General"'.

Other articles in the press book contained statements such as the following: 'the gallant engineer yearned for glory in the first line of fighting'; 'fearing for the safety of his beloved locomotive … and to rescue his sweetheart, a prisoner of the foe, [he] pursues [the raiders]'; '[i]n his role of a young Confederate fire-eater, Buster pursues the northerners'.[160] Regardless of the film's actual content, at least some of the press book's writers were inclined to think that Johnnie Gray is a gung-ho patriot eager to enlist and fight; that he finds out why he was turned away by the recruiters; that his particularly strong attachment to his engine is a consequence of having been rejected by his girlfriend; that his pursuit of the stolen engine also has the objective of rescuing his sweetheart; and that he is looking for glory. These misleading claims and assumptions point to the fact that the apparently so straightforward story of *The General* is unusual enough to confuse these writers.

The potential for confusion is already there in the film's title. One article in the press book, entitled 'Buster Keaton Not "The General" After All', explained that, while one would normally assume the title character to be played by the star, here the title referred to 'the crack railway snorter of Big Shanty', whereas 'Buster plays the part of the young engineer'. Yet, elsewhere, the press book encouraged a different interpretation of the title; in several advertisements, Keaton's character is portrayed wearing a Confederate officer's uniform. Of course, before going to see *The General*, those audience members who had read articles about the film, or knew the historical event it was based upon, probably realised that its title referred to a locomotive. More fundamentally, cinemagoers familiar with Keaton's previous films would find it hard to believe that the comedian was playing a general. In most of his features up to this point, Keaton's character starts out either as a pampered, rich youth who is (initially) unable to function in the wider world (as in *The Navigator* and *Battling Butler*)[161] or a rather average, perhaps below-average, young man with little money, few skills and unpromising career prospects (as in *Three Ages*, *Sherlock Jr.* and *Go West*). In *Our Hospitality*, Willie McKay seems to be a perfectly respectable member of Northern society, but he is out of his depths when he arrives in the South. Only in *Seven Chances* does Keaton start out as a middle-class professional (a broker); however, his firm is on the verge of bankruptcy.

In the course of these films, the protagonist reveals unexpected strength, skill and ingenuity (in *Sherlock Jr.*, he does so only in a dream), which put him in a position where he can finally be with the woman he loves. But in none of Keaton's previous features does his character attain an important position in the world of work. He only dreams of becoming a famous detective in *Sherlock Jr.* (after his real-life detecting has backfired) but remains a lowly cinema employee, responsible for projecting films and cleaning up the theatre. He never gets an actual job in *The Navigator* and *Battling Butler*, nor is there any mention of a career at the end of *Our Hospitality* and the three stories in *Three Ages*. His future work role on the cattle ranch of his prospective father-in-law in *Go West* remains undefined, and he still lacks conventional cowboy skills at the end. In *Seven Chances*, he is only just able to prevent bankruptcy with an inheritance. In the light of these earlier films, then, prospective viewers of *The General* would have found it highly unlikely, irrespective of their prior knowledge about the film, that Keaton starts out as a general, or rises to this eminent rank by the end.

And yet the film's title and some of the advertisements indicated that this Keaton film might be different, that this time his character would turn out to be a traditional hero and be recognised as such by everyone in the world of the film's story, the uniform confirming his exalted status. Indeed, such an outcome would fit into the trajectory of the three previous Buster Keaton Productions releases, in which the title appears to identify the character he plays. In *Sherlock Jr.*, Keaton's character can live up to the expectations raised by the title only in his dreams, while in *The Navigator* – an earlier example of a title referring to a vehicle (here an ocean liner) rather than a character – he never learns to navigate, but he does manage to adapt to life on-board a drifting ship. And in *Battling Butler*, Keaton plays a character who, after only pretending to be the 'Battling Butler' of the title, does eventually get into a brutal fight with the boxer so named, from which he emerges victorious. In other words, across the endings of these three films, the Keaton character gets ever closer to becoming the person that the title promises him to be.

The implicit question raised by the title of *The General* is, then, whether the Keaton character can finally grow into the role suggested by it. At the same time, most information circulating about the film in the press stated explicitly that his character was defined by his professional and emotional attachment to an engine called General. Thus, we could say that prospective viewers were encouraged to approach screenings of *The General* with somewhat contradictory expectations about Keaton's role in it – a dedicated locomotive engineer *and* a potential military hero. Not coincidentally, this is, of course, the very tension underpinning the film's story. Annabelle expects Johnnie to join the army rather than continuing what he does best and is happy with – and also, in the judgment of the Southern general, what he is most useful at in times of war. By the end of the film, the Southern general has revised his opinion about Johnnie's value for the South as an engineer and makes him a lieutenant (not quite a general, but at least an officer), which Annabelle is very happy about, although one has to wonder whether she and Johnnie have thought through the implications of his enlistment.

Let's take a closer look at *The General*'s beginning and its ending. The film's character and cast list includes *five* generals ('General Thatcher', 'A Southern General', 'Three Union Generals'). The name of Keaton's character – 'Johnnie Gray' – evokes the gray/grey uniform of the Confederacy, but he has no rank, unlike all the generals and 'Captain Anderson'. The remaining three characters are, like Johnnie, listed as civilians ('Annabelle Lee', 'Her father', 'Her brother'), yet their last name calls to mind the most famous of Confederate generals (Robert E. Lee). So, before the story even begins, Johnnie is deeply immersed in a military world.

After the conclusion of the credits, an expository intertitle situates the story which is about to unfold geographically ('Marietta, Ga.') and temporally ('the Spring of 1861'), while also describing the object which is to be seen ('[t]he Western and Atlantic Flyer') and its activity ('speeding into Marietta'). The following extreme long shot shows a train moving at what for twentieth-century audiences would appear to be a rather leisurely pace, thus alerting viewers that they will have to adjust some of their expectations (with regards, for example, to how fast a 'speeding' 'Flyer' moves in the early 1860s). A cut to a medium long shot, tracking parallel to the moving train, shows Keaton at the controls of its engine, and then reveals that the name of this locomotive is 'General'. Those (probably very few) viewers who thought that the film's title referred to Keaton's character are thus shown how wrong they were.

However, those viewers who suspected or knew all along that Keaton would not appear in the role of a general also have to adjust their expectations somewhat in the opening sequence. Unlike Keaton's previous features, in this one his character has a crucial role to play in the local community (a small crowd of people await his train's arrival and a larger number of passengers then disembark, several of them waving to Johnnie); he also has authority (he gives orders to his assistant) and is much admired (two boys approach him upon his arrival and follow his every move; see p. 70). In other words, he is the kind of man that a young Southern lady and her family would

welcome as a suitor. This contrasts sharply with the opening
sequences of his previous features, which reveal his character's lowly
social status, his inappropriate behaviour and/or his ignorance and
lack of crucial skills – in other words, everything that disqualifies him
as a suitor. By comparison, the beginning of *The General* feels more
like an ending: having proven and established himself in the wider
world, Johnnie can finally ask his girlfriend to marry him.

After an intertitle has identified the 'two loves in his life' and
Johnnie has put Annabelle's picture, which hangs in his cab, into his
coat pocket (because he wants to be close to her at all times), he
confidently walks to her house. Seemingly with something important
on his mind (perhaps today he will finally propose), he is unaware
that the two boys are following him, as is Annabelle, who falls in
line behind them. When he reaches her front door, he is surprised to
find that he has company but quickly recovers his composure, and
once inside tries to focus on the business at hand again, sitting down

with Annabelle on a settee, with the boys seated nearby (in a sense, they represent the children the couple will soon have if the courtship results, as one would expect at this point, in marriage).

Whatever Johnnie came to do is too personal to be done in the presence of the boys, though, and he marches them out again (pretending to leave, but then closing the door behind them). He sits down once more and gives Annabelle a picture, which shows him standing in front of the General. He wants her, through this picture, to have him in her house at all times and also to acknowledge that he is inseparable from his engine, and she accepts this by displaying it prominently on the little table in the centre of the room. Standing at the table, she looks at him, while Johnnie – still sitting on the settee – looks up at her. This is a moment where he might quite easily slide from his sitting position onto his knees and propose.

But at this point the film begins to move in a different direction with a cut to her father looking out of the window in another room. Next, both the father and the person he saw outside (his son) invade the space of the two young lovers. Johnnie and Annabelle sit close to each other, looking into each other's eyes, but then turn to become spectators to the exchange between father and son about the outbreak of war. The son wants 'to be one of the first to enlist', and the father decides to go with him. Annabelle stands up to say goodbye to them, while Johnnie remains seated, his eyes on her.

She comes back to stand directly in front of him, so that once again
he is in a position where he could get on his knees to propose – but
this is not what she has in mind, as the next intertitle makes clear:
'Aren't you going to enlist?' Up to this question, it was still
thinkable that, given the fact that Annabelle will soon be alone in
the house (with her father and brother away at war and no mother
in sight), this would be the right moment for Johnnie to ask her to
become his wife so that he could always be there for her. But the
romantic narrative convention of young women expecting their
suitors to propose to them is here displaced by a patriotic narrative
about women sending their men off to war (which, in this case, also
means that Johnnie will have to give up his job and be separated
from his beloved engine).

Johnnie is not at all prepared for this turn of events.
He is flustered, unsure about how to proceed and positively
uncoordinated when Annabelle gives him a goodbye kiss – after

which he strikes an incongruous dramatic farewell pose and falls down. He then races to the recruitment office, his attempt to be the very first in line a result less of his belief in the rightness of the cause than his perceived need to compensate for his late, and indeed somewhat reluctant, start. He seems to feel that only by being outwardly more eager than anyone else can he convince others (and himself) that he really wants to be a soldier. Inside the office, he immediately gets sidetracked by following a clerk away from the actual recruiter, as if, deep down, he never intended to enlist in the first place.

During the remainder of the film, Johnnie makes many mistakes – because he is under enormous pressure, too focused on the task at hand to notice what is going on around him, subjected to the noise of his engine, or otherwise hampered by adverse external circumstances or a distracted frame of mind – but the worst of these mistakes occur when he takes on a military role. While pursuing the General, he comes across a cannon and immediately gets the idea to use it against the stolen train, which is an appropriate action in the context of war, but makes little sense here. After all, he still thinks that the train has been stolen by deserters, rather than by enemy spies, and he also loves the engine he is now trying to shoot at. He almost gets *himself* pulverised by the cannon ball (which has a certain logic, because aiming the cannon at his beloved engine is like shooting himself), and it is only a lucky coincidence that it flies past him and explodes just behind the stolen train.

When, in Part 5, Johnnie picks up a sword in Dalton to complete his military outfit and runs after the departing Confederate army, he immediately gets this new piece of equipment entangled between his legs and falls down. During the battle, he mimics the gestures of the Union general to no real purpose, and when doing so the blade of his sword keeps flying off the handle. Trying to pick it up, he almost gets himself killed again by a Confederate cannon, but then, by sheer coincidence, like the cannon ball in Part 2, his blade eventually does some good by flying off and killing a Union sniper. When, subsequently, he takes charge of a cannon and fires it straight up into the air, he is rightly worried that the projectile will come down and hit him – yet, through another amazing coincidence, it lands on a nearby dam. And, as mentioned before, when, at the end of the battle, he grabs the Confederate flag, he is immediately upended by the officer he is standing on. Johnnie's actions in the battle scene have deadly consequences, but they are in effect like a child's play-acting – more specifically, a little boy's attempt to act like a man. The film has some fun with what in retrospect we might call phallic imagery, as when Johnnie holds his sword at his crotch, only to have the blade drop off later on; or when the cannon points, somewhat obscenely framed by two wheels, straight up; or, indeed, when Johnnie himself stands erect with the Confederate flag, only then to be knocked over by a real (military) man.

After the battle, an intertitle announces the arrival of the '[h]eroes of the day' in Dalton, with Johnnie marching next to the general, yet soon stepping aside to let the real soldiers receive their heroes' welcome. He knows that he is not one of them (among other things, he never finds out that he accidentally killed a sniper and destroyed the dam) and that instead he belongs to his engine, which is where he goes. However, upon finding the Union general in the cab of the General, he has to hand him over to the Southern commander. While he does his best to follow military procedure, he disrupts the Union general's surrender by accidentally discharging his gun, confirming that he simply cannot be trusted with a role in the army and its associated weaponry. When the Southern commander sternly enquires about the uniform he is wearing and then orders him to take it off, Johnnie sadly, but without any resistance, accepts that this is what he has to do, because he is not in fact a soldier.

It takes him quite a long time to figure out that the coat and hat he is given belong to an officer's uniform. He gets very excited about this, especially when he realises that Annabelle and her father are watching him, happy about this unexpected turn of events. As soon as Annabelle rushes over to him, he strikes what is in this context a rather ridiculous pose. When he is finally being enlisted, he responds (in his only medium close-up in the film, close-ups being absent altogether) to the question about his occupation with the word 'soldier', thus denying both his true identity as an engineer and his love for the General. Johnnie has become so caught up in other people's expectations (most notably those of Annabelle and her father) and in military play-acting that he has lost sight of who he really is and what he really wants.

For all we know, he never figured out why he was originally refused enlistment, in the same way that Annabelle never found out that she wronged Johnnie when rejecting him for having failed to enlist at the beginning of the film, or that he did not in fact enter enemy territory just to save her. So their reunion at the end of the

film is built on very shaky foundations. Indeed, when they sit down on the General's drive rod, it is a poignant reminder of Annabelle's previous failure to trust Johnnie and her unfair rejection of him. And when their kissing is interrupted by saluting soldiers walking past, this foreshadows what Johnnie will have to do in the not too distant future, which is to leave Annabelle and the General to go into battle with the rest of the army, where it is very likely (as demonstrated by the injuries sustained by Annabelle's father and brother) that he will be wounded, maybe even killed.

This understanding of the film's conclusion is supported by a closer look at the ending of *Our Hospitality*, Keaton's only previous film about Southern society. Whereas in *The General*, the girl's father and brother decide to go to war at the earliest opportunity, thus raising expectations for Johnnie to do the same (with the likely prospect of getting injured or killed), in *Our Hospitality* the girl's father and two brothers directly attack Willie McKay because they feel obliged to continue a feud from decades past. But the code of Southern hospitality requires them to suspend all hostilities while he is a guest in their house. Willie stays as long as possible, but eventually feels the need to escape, which leads not only to a chase but also to his spectacular rescue of Virginia Canfield at a waterfall. However, he cannot count on the Canfields' gratitude (for one thing, they did not witness the rescue) and calculates that marrying Virginia in their house might doubly protect him (in addition to being their guest, he is now also a member of the family). Indeed, the Canfield men finally lay down their weapons and reluctantly accept him – at which point Willie reveals that he was prepared for a more hostile turn of events, with an arsenal of weapons hidden on his body. The film thus paints a grim picture of Southern culture, where violence is always prone to erupt, encouraging the Keaton character to prepare for and, if necessary, engage in violence as well – which is also what happens in *The General*.

It is possible to understand the endings of both *Our Hospitality* and *The General* in a different way, insofar as the two films could be seen to endorse violence as an essential aspect of masculine identity. However, this kind of interpretation is actively discouraged by the ending of *Battling Butler*. Here, Alfred Butler's deception is punished by the real Battling Butler in his dressing room, yet, with his wife looking on, Alfred fights back and eventually knocks out the boxer. He then admits to his wife: 'I'm not even a real fighter.' Of course, he has just shown that he can be, and this demonstration could be the basis for the story's resolution, with his wife saying something like 'But you are!' Instead she says, 'I'm glad', thus rejecting the assumption that violence is, or should be, a crucial aspect of Alfred's identity, or the only way that he can prove his manliness.

This would seem to confirm the interpretation of the ending of *The General* I have proposed. That Johnnie, under pressure from his girlfriend and her family and a militaristic Southern society, becomes convinced that he has to be a soldier and in the process lays the foundation for becoming separated, temporarily, perhaps even permanently, from the 'two loves' of his life without even realising it is nothing short of tragic.[162] One could take this argument even further, insofar as the film highlights the potential decisiveness of the Union's military offensive; once over the Rock River bridge, 'nothing on earth' could have stopped it, which implies that the war might have been won by Union forces right then. But Johnnie's bridge burning, his warning of the Confederate army and his accidental destruction of a dam during the battle force the Union army to retreat, thus, in the logic of the film, it would seem, prolonging the deadliest war in American history by three years.

Having closely examined the film's beginning and ending, in the next chapter I discuss the rest of *The General*, with a particular focus on style, and how it contributes to the attractions on display in the film and to the story it tells about Johnnie's unique interaction with machinery and human beings.

7 Style, Spectacle and Story

The press book for *The General* contained several advertisements for the film which cinema managers could place in local newspapers (presumably the same designs were used by the distributor to promote the film in the regional and national press). The overall focus of these advertisements was on the promise of laughter: 'You'll darn near fall off your seat as Buster rolls up one tremendous laugh moment after another,' predicted one ad, while another simply declared: 'Laughter Guaranteed'. The laughter was deemed to be so explosive that it could damage one's health: 'Warning to our patrons! ... The Management will not be responsible for ribs bent, broken, wrecked or split, caused by over-laughing, over-shaking or uncontrolled hilarity.'

The prospective viewer's body would not only be shaken by laughter but also by other kinds of extreme physical excitement: 'You are going to gasp and shake, shiver and quiver at [Buster's] thrilling rides and daring adventures.' Indeed, most ads promised both 'laughs' and 'thrills': 'Laughs that last. Thrills that chill'; 'the biggest laugh and thrill show [Buster Keaton] ever made'. The majority of ad designs tied these prospective physical responses to train rides and military conflict, which were evoked both in drawings and in the text. In several pictures, Johnnie – always drawn with a serious demeanour and mostly in uniform – is fired upon by a cannon and pursued by soldiers while riding a train (both with and without a woman holding on to him). The comedian is 'the Laughter Leader[,] [t]he General of Joy'. And the film itself is compared to a train, with the audience being invited to hop on: 'Choo! Choo! The Laughter Special's Here! ... Come ride with [Buster Keaton]!'

When compared to the film's main selling points as presented across the rest of the press book, it is noticeable that the advertisements failed to foreground *The General*'s big budget, its Civil War setting, the fact that it was based on a well-known historical event and its striving for historical accuracy. Instead, they focused almost exclusively on Keaton's characteristic performance style (his reduced facial expressivity is explicitly referenced, while his acrobatics are only implied) and on exciting as well as comical action associated with the intersection of train rides and warfare (whereby the large scale of the film's action was only hinted at). Most insistently, the advertisements promised prospective viewers an extraordinarily intense physical response to the film, in the form of laughter and the kind of agitation here referred to as 'thrills'.

It was a risky strategy to promise such intensity, because audiences – even those having a perfectly satisfactory experience – might well be disappointed when their actual response to the film fell short of what they had been 'guaranteed'; indeed, judging by the reviews of the film discussed in the Introduction, many people felt this way. Also, by playing up physical reactions, the ads did not prepare audiences for the importance of primarily mental (emotional as well as cognitive) responses to the film – in particular to the protagonist's feelings, to the cleverness of many of his actions and of the film's overall design, to the beauty of the settings and the compelling evocation of a historically distant world. There was, potentially, so much else to be enjoyed and appreciated beyond the ads' focus on laughs and thrills.

Yet it was not just the advertising's all too narrow focus which got in the way of contemporary audience's full enjoyment and appreciation of the film. As previously noted, many commentators at the time felt that Keaton's reduced facial expressivity made it difficult for audiences to perceive his on-screen performance as that of a fully fledged character with whom they could empathise. This problem was magnified by the preponderance of long shots (showing the actors' full bodies in the frame) and extreme long shots (in which the surroundings dwarf the actors' bodies), and the complete absence of close-ups (in which an actor's face fills the frame), as well as the

extreme rarity of medium close-ups (showing face and chest), and
also the scarcity of dialogue and expository intertitles (there are,
for example, only seven in Part 2b and five in Part 4).

While the film's many extreme long shots contribute to the
distancing of the audience from Johnnie, they also fulfil important
positive functions. The very first shot after the opening intertitle
puts the landscape and the long train passing through it on display.
This could be considered as nothing more than a conventional
establishing shot, yet the film frequently features shots in which
landscapes and massive sets dwarf the human figures, as when the
General arrives in Marietta or when Johnnie, the two boys and
Annabelle approach her house. The train's arrival at Big Shanty is
similarly staged and filmed in a way that shows off the train and the
town set. Later on, extreme long shots depict one train going past
another on converging tracks (in Big Shanty, in Part 2) and three
trains next to each other on parallel tracks (in Part 4). In some
shots, individuals get lost in a sea of people, as when the Union
army advances towards Johnnie's train in Part 2, when the
Confederate army leaves Dalton and when the Union army
approaches, and then retreats from, the climactic battle (both in
Part 5). The most spectacular locations or sets presented in extreme
long shots are the massive bridge from which the raiders drop
planks onto the Texas passing through underneath (in Part 2);

the huge train depot and Union army camp near Chattanooga; the Rock River bridge, especially when it collapses under the weight of the Texas; and the explosion of the dam (all in Part 4).

The purpose of these extreme long shots (many of which also *last* quite a long time) is manifold. They display the beauty of the film's locations and the impressive size of its sets, props, cast and action, at the same time assuring spectators that what they see really did happen in front of the camera (rather than being the result of trick photography and editing), which also might, together with the historically accurate recreation of the look of the Civil War era (in terms of costumes, props and sets), enhance their impression of being transported into the past. Somewhat closer shots are often

used to depict the movement of trains, with the camera running on
a parallel track at the same speed, so that the train and the people
on it remain fixed in the frame, while the background rushes past –
as when Johnnie moves past the retreating Confederate army in
Part 2. Alternatively, the camera is placed on the train itself. In both
cases, a strong sense of movement is conveyed to the audience.
This applies to much of Parts 2b and 4.

   In addition, both long shots and extreme long shots are used
to give a comprehensive and clear picture of the spatial layout of the
action and thus to explain why it turns out the way it does. For
example, the cannon Johnnie has commandeered in Part 2 and its
relationship both to the Texas and the General is captured in a single

shot, which also reveals the curve on the track that ensures the Texas is out of harm's way when the cannon fires. Apart from presenting broad overviews of how people, vehicles, tracks, bridges and towns are laid out in relation to each other, the film pays particular attention to Johnnie's physical interaction with the world around him. Here, the emphasis is very much on trains and other vehicles.

Johnnie's very first appearance in the film shows him in the cab of the General, and he ends Part 1 sitting dejectedly on its drive rod, only belatedly noticing that his assistant has set the engine in motion so as to move it (and with it Johnnie) into a shed. During much of the remainder of the film, Johnnie is alternately in charge of vehicles or involuntarily subjected to their movements. For example, in Part 2 he vigorously and confidently rides a handcar until it gets derailed and throws him off. He then sees a bicycle and, in one fluid motion, jumps on its seat and takes off, only to lose balance soon thereafter. Once he has taken charge of the Texas, he is forced to run in front of the train so as to clear the track. Having picked up one heavy wooden plank, he gets caught on the train's cow-catcher and is seemingly incapacitated. However, when the train's progress is blocked by another obstacle, he manages to remove it with the help of the plank he picked up first (see p. 86). Later on, he is too preoccupied to realise that the raiders have thrown a switch to divert his train onto an unfinished side track; he manages to stop it at the last possible moment. Back on the

main track, the engine's wheels lose traction, and he has to get off to throw dirt under them; however, Johnnie is too focused on kicking loose more dirt to realise that the train has started moving again – and when he finally does, he has to run fast to catch up.

Thus, Parts 2b and 4, as well as the beginning and end of Part 1, focus on Johnnie's interaction with moving vehicles – driving them, sitting down on them, running on top of them, chasing after them. In the process, Johnnie displays his athleticism and problem-solving skills but also reveals his tendency – which is perfectly understandable in the high-pressure circumstances of the chase, during which he has to make do without his assistant – to overlook key elements of the situations he finds himself in.[163] This creates new problems that he is then promptly able to solve. Once again, the use of (extreme) long shots in these sequences both makes it easy for spectators to understand exactly how and why things happen, and assures them that the action, including Keaton's stunts, did indeed take place in front of the camera.[164]

Much of the interaction between Keaton and his various vehicles could be regarded as funny – giving rise to the kind of laughter the advertisements promised – or as thrilling, insofar as Johnnie is constantly threatened with disaster, only avoiding it very narrowly. But it is equally possible to be amazed by, or simply to appreciate, the cleverness of the overall design of the action, Keaton's athleticism or his character's ability to solve all problems.

There is a particularly interesting example of clever design in Part 2. In this sequence, Johnnie steers the train car left behind by the raiders onto a side track, which then, without him noticing, reconnects with the main track, so that the car he thought he had disposed of shows up in front of him again. A medium shot reveals

his surprise (his mouth is open, his eyes are wide) and his thought process: he closes his eyes, thinking perhaps that the car he sees is just an illusion, but when he reopens them and the car is still there, he turns around to look back to where he came from; if the car he pushed on the side track is still on it, then the one in front of him must be a different one – but, of course, it is not; he closes his eyes once more. There is no reverse shot showing what Johnnie has seen. Next, Johnnie is distracted by steam escaping from a valve, and when he looks out front again, the car is gone, because, unbeknownst to him, it has been derailed. Once more, a medium shot reveals his reaction, which is similar to the one before, except that now Johnnie is also looking left and right to see whether something on the side of the track might explain the mystery. And again, there is no reverse shot. The focus stays on Johnnie's face and torso throughout, and on the thoughts animating them.

The use of medium shots in this sequence makes it stand out from most of the rest of the film (while the absence of reverse shots is, as we will see, quite typical). Indeed, the film playfully highlights its avoidance of close shots by including early on a close-up portrait of Annabelle in a small frame within the film's larger frame. In Part 3, her face is also singled out in a point-of-view shot, as seen by Johnnie through the hole that was burnt into the table cloth behind which he is hiding in the Union headquarters; once again we have a small (in this case even tiny) frame within the larger frame of the film, a close-up that is a long distance away – and therefore not a close-up at all. By contrast, the shots of Johnnie's eye looking through the hole would be genuine close-ups if the rest of his face was not hidden by the cloth.

The almost complete absence of close shots goes hand in hand with the relative scarcity of cut-ins and shot/reverse-shot sequences. Johnnie is often shown looking intently at something or someone, either in the same frame or off screen. But there are a few occasions when a closer shot emphasises what he is looking at, or when the film cuts back and forth between Johnnie and the person or object

he is concerned with. This is strikingly illustrated by the sequence
from Part 2 discussed on pp. 87–8 and by Johnnie's response to
being kicked out of the recruitment office by the Southern general in
Part 1. He looks straight at the camera (here taking the place of the
general, who was shown in the preceding long shot standing
opposite Johnnie) and speaks, his words appearing on the intertitle
('If you lose this war, don't blame me') – but the reverse shot
showing the general to whom his words are addressed is missing.

When the film does employ shot/reverse-shot constructions,
Johnnie's orientation in the frame is often such that he does not
appear to look at the person he is interacting with. For example,
when the recruiter, who is looking up to the right in a very rare
medium close-up, asks for his name, Johnnie is shown, in a medium
shot, staring straight ahead so that he is not actually facing the
recruiter. When Johnnie soon afterwards tries to enlist again, he hides
his face behind a hat and pretends to be someone else; now the
medium close-up of the recruiter and the dialogue intertitle are
followed by a medium shot of Johnnie looking down and to the left –
but his view of the recruiter is blocked by the hat he is hiding behind.

The overall effect of all this is that, while Johnnie is physically
integrated into his surroundings – as highlighted by long shots and
extreme long shots – he is, in many situations, communicatively and
emotionally detached from other people, due to the rarity of close

shots, cut-ins and reverse shots, or because his look off screen is blocked or misdirected. The film thus shifts emphasis away from Johnnie's looks and emotions to his situatedness in physical environments, to his perception and understanding of his physical relationship with the people and objects around him, and to his physical interaction with them.

Most importantly, Parts 3–6 emphasise Johnnie's physical interaction with Annabelle. In a sense, Part 3 picks up on the courtship story that was interrupted and displaced in Part 1. Then the expectation was that (eventually) Johnnie would propose and get married to Annabelle; now he enters her bedroom and does indeed spend the night with her. Johnnie first clamps his hand over

her mouth, then grabs her body to move it through the window,
after which he tries (with only intermittent success) to hold on to
her hand while running around in the forest, until finally he sits
down, holding her in his arms, and goes to sleep. In Chapter 5,
I examined the many ways in which the events of the story
conspire to punish Annabelle for her previous rejection of
Johnnie. What I have not so far discussed is how well, despite
some misunderstandings and mishaps, they work together in
Part 4 and how much domestic imagery and sexual tension
intrude on their adventure, and also how the various 'mistakes'
they make can be understood as the expression of a veritable battle
of the sexes.[165]

Towards the beginning of Part 4, despite being uncomfortably
confined in a sack, Annabelle is able to uncouple the back of the
train so that they can speedily take off with the General. After
Johnnie has liberated her from the sack, they get very intimate
when he moves her out of the boxcar. Quite surprisingly, she then
immediately shows some initiative; while Johnnie stops and loads
up more firewood, Annabelle ties a rope between two trees across
the railroad. Returning to the cab of the General, she ignores the
helping hand Johnnie offers her, and climbs up all on her own.
Although Johnnie was not impressed by her rope, it does slow down
the pursuers. Afterwards, when the couple try to fill up the water

tank, Johnnie's mistakes result in a thorough drenching for Annabelle. There is considerable latent aggression in this scene, and it is sexually charged. This dimension of their interaction is made explicit in their next scene.

During a lull in the action, Annabelle starts behaving as if the General's cab was their home. When Johnnie asks her to feed the woodburner, she throws away a log because it has a hole, and then proceeds to sweep the cab until an exasperated Johnnie pulls the broom away from her and tells her to continue firing the engine. She does so with a little stick of wood. In disbelief, Johnnie picks up a tiny splinter and hands it to her. After she dutifully puts it in the burner, he throttles her – and then kisses her (see p. 94). This kiss echoes the one she gave him when he left her house for the recruitment office. On that occasion, she had just derailed their courtship by demanding that he goes to war; now Johnnie's kiss confirms that, despite everything she has done, he still loves her.

Annabelle then makes a number of mistakes that get Johnnie into trouble (instead of just exasperating him); in a sense, she is fighting back. Johnnie asks her to operate the engine while he ties a chain to a switch so that the train's forward movement bends it all out of shape. But she is unable to stop the train, which forces him to charge down a hill in pursuit; by the time he gets to the bottom, she has finally worked out how to stop and reverse, which means that he has to race up the hill again. Later, on the Rock River bridge, Johnnie stops the train, gets out and asks her to hand down the wood he needs to build a pile, which he intends to set alight with the kerosene from the train's lantern. When she gives him an all-too-small piece, he throws it right back at her. Soon thereafter, she accidentally pushes a piece of burning wood onto the pile, which immediately catches fire, stranding Johnnie on the wrong side. He gets ready to jump across the flames, hoping to be able to hold on to the train, but Annabelle has in the meantime moved it, so that he falls through the bridge into the river. Each of them has managed to get the other one really wet once; they are now even. When Johnnie is subsequently shot at by a Confederate soldier, it is Annabelle who realises that it is because of his Northern uniform. She helps him change, which is a very wifely as well as homely thing to do. And with this, Part 4 ends.

Once again, there are plenty of potential laughs and thrills in this part of the film, but, as I have tried to show, it is perhaps best understood as an exploration of Johnnie and Annabelle's relationship, an exploration focusing on collaborative action, gestures and physical contact shown in long shots, rather than on facial expressions, looks and emotional connections presented in closer shots. Indeed, I have suggested that some of their most powerful feelings for each other are expressed through mistakes and violence. While this is certainly a rather unusual depiction of a romantic relationship, in the context of the film's story, Johnnie and Annabelle's journey in Part 4 is a kind of utopian moment, in which Johnnie is united with the woman and the engine he loves; the General serves as a place of work and a home (due especially to Annabelle's efforts to treat it as such), and Johnnie is both doing the job he loves and carrying out a military mission.

As discussed in the previous chapter, this moment does not last. The film's final image of a uniformed Johnnie cleverly positioning himself on the General in such a way that he can kiss Annabelle while also saluting the soldiers walking past recreates the magic of their journey. But it is also very ominous, because, like the soldiers, Johnnie will eventually have to exit the frame so as to confront what is, quite possibly, 'The End'.

Conclusion

The General was announced as Buster Keaton's 'first independent film', because 'he is now one of the United Artists', the company having originally been set up as an alternative to the major studios (especially Paramount).[166] Keaton's previous features had been *made* independently by Buster Keaton Productions but had been *distributed* by one of the majors (Metro/MGM). Despite the switch from MGM to United Artists, *The General* was to be premiered – probably as a consequence of a special arrangement between Joseph Schenck and his brother, Nicholas – in MGM's flagship cinema in New York, the Capitol, which was said to be the largest movie theatre in the world. Because *Flesh and the Devil* (1926), a romantic drama featuring two of MGM's biggest stars (John Gilbert and Greta Garbo) was doing exceptionally well at the Capitol, the premiere of *The General* was delayed from mid-January 1927 until 5 February.[167]

The Capitol's programme on that day opened with the 'Northern Rhapsody' played by the 'Capitol Grand Orchestra'.[168] This overture lasted 12 minutes and was followed by a 7-minute German documentary entitled *Soaring Wings*, the performance on the Capitol's stage of the Irving Berlin song 'What Does It Matter?' and the theatre's own newsreel, the 8-minute *Capitol Magazine*. Next came another stage performance, a dance number entitled 'Milady's Boudoir', which lasted 9 minutes and involved, among others, the 'Capitol Ballet Corps' and the 'Chester Hale Girls'. Finally, after almost forty minutes of support acts, *The General* was shown, with musical accompaniment from the orchestra. When the screening was over, people left the auditorium to the sounds of the 'Capitol Grand Organ'.[169]

This was not a special programme put on for the premiere of *The General*; it was the usual way in which films were presented in movie palaces at that time (whereas smaller cinemas could not afford many live performers and instead were likely to show more short films, accompanied by only a few musicians or a single pianist).[170] And this kind of presentation was important to reviewers. When the *New York Times* reviewed *The General*, a third of the text was dedicated to the support acts, praising the 'excellent scenes of the riots in Hankow, China' included in the newsreel, while *Soaring Wings* was judged to be 'absorbing'.[171] Half of the review in the *Philadelphia Inquirer* dealt with the live performances preceding *The General* at the Fox Theatre; indeed, it declared that 'the outstanding feature' of the evening's programme was not Keaton's movie but 'the beautiful adagio dancing by Fred Easter and Ruth Hazleton'.[172]

Thus, United Artists managed to get bookings for *The General* on the major theatre circuits, but the film did not perform particularly well. After years of steadily increasing revenues for Keaton's features, *The General*'s domestic rentals of $486,500 were in the same range as the earnings of the first three features released by Buster Keaton Productions back in 1923–4.[173] The 1926 distribution contract between Buster Keaton Productions and United Artists (which was in many ways more advantageous for Keaton's studio than its contract with MGM had been) stipulated that the former would receive 75 per cent of domestic rentals and between 60 and 70 per cent of foreign earnings, without any advance being paid by the distributor.[174] Thus, Buster Keaton Productions' share of domestic rentals for *The General* was $365,000 and, if we assume once again that foreign earnings were about a quarter of the total, its share of those was about $110,000. This adds up to $475,000. The fact that there was only a small profit of about $60,000 ($475,000 minus the film's $415,000 budget) for Buster Keaton Productions was a huge disappointment but not a catastrophe. However, the distributor's share of domestic rentals would have been only about $120,000, with around $50,000 to be added from foreign earnings; assuming that United Artists' distribution costs were as high as elsewhere in the industry (that is, several hundred thousand dollars for a film such as *The General*),[175] this meant that the company lost money.

For Joseph Schenck, who was in charge of both Buster Keaton Productions and United Artists, this was a serious problem. Things got worse when Keaton's next film, *College*, released in September 1927, had domestic rentals of only $440,000, making a solid profit for Buster Keaton Productions (because it cost only $290,000 to make) but causing the distributor a further loss.[176] What is more, in a listing of the twelve films released by United Artists in 1927, *College* and *The General* came second and third from the bottom in terms of domestic rentals.[177] With much else going on in the film industry (not least the introduction of pre-recorded synchronised sound, initially only used in a few cinemas for some short films and the orchestral accompaniment of selected features, but soon to lead to the extraordinarily expensive wholesale technological conversion of all film studios and movie theatres),[178] Schenck decided that after completing *Steamboat Bill, Jr.*, which was the final film of Keaton's 1924 employment contract with Buster Keaton Productions, the comedian should move from his independent studio to MGM.[179]

In the light of the rather poor performance of his two most recent films, it is somewhat surprising to find that the employment contract Keaton signed with MGM on 26 January 1928 stipulated a salary of $150,000 per year (that is, almost $3,000 per week).[180] One suspects that Joseph Schenck had once again turned to his brother to arrange this lucrative deal for his brother-in-law – after all, as we have seen before, Hollywood was very much a family affair. As far as Keaton's career is concerned, a new chapter began in 1928, while the previous one was finally closed with the release, in May 1928, of *Steamboat Bill, Jr.* – arguably one of Keaton's finest films, and also his biggest flop.[181]

By the end of the following year, Keaton was singing and dancing in his first musical film, *The Hollywood Revue of 1929* –

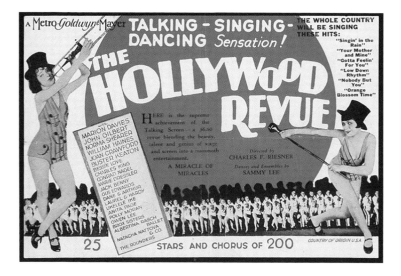

thus, somewhat ironically, returning to the very format he had rejected in favour of film-making when leaving the Shuberts' stage revue *The Passing Show of 1917* behind to join Comique twelve years earlier. By the time *The Hollywood Revue of 1929* was released in November 1929, many American film studios and movie theatres had converted to sound. From then on, there was a rapidly shrinking market for re-releases of silent films, unless they were upgraded with a musical soundtrack and sound effects (and possibly a voiceover), as happened with *The Birth of a Nation* in the 1930s,[182] and, most famously, with *The Gold Rush* in 1942.[183]

Sound versions were created for films that, like *The Birth of a Nation* and *The Gold Rush*, had been huge hits and could be assumed to have continuing popular appeal in mainstream movie theatres. As we have seen, *The General* did not belong to this category. So, for many years the film was only shown, very occasionally, at film societies, festivals and specialised (repertory or art-house) cinemas. At one such rare screening at the Coronet Theatre in Hollywood which Keaton himself attended in 1954, he met the cinema's manager Raymond Rohauer, who then took it upon himself to work with Keaton on finding good prints of his films and bringing them back into movie theatres (often after some re-editing).[184] First, Rohauer prepared a sound version of *The General* featuring music and sound effects, and also, curiously, replacing the intertitles with superimposed text so that the dialogue, for example, would be superimposed on shots of the speakers.[185] In 1962, a hundred years after the historical Andrews raid (which had also been the subject of Disney's 1956 movie *The Great Locomotive Chase*), Keaton toured West Germany and Austria with this new version of *The General*.[186]

By then, the reputation of his silent films, especially *The General*, had started to grow, soon to match – even eclipse – that of Chaplin's work. In the 1950s and early 60s, film critics and historians had started interviewing Keaton about his work during the silent era, with some of these interviews being published in specialist film journals.[187] He had been the subject of a Hollywood biopic, *The Buster Keaton Story* (1957), which introduces him as 'one of the immortals of the silent screen', and in 1960 he had published his autobiography *My Wonderful World of Slapstick*, while also receiving a special Academy Award 'for his unique talents which brought immortal comedies to the screen'.[188]

Whereas, in the 1950s, Chaplin's movies (especially *The Gold Rush*) had come close to dominating surveys of international critical opinion about the best films ever made,[189] in the 1960s and 70s they had to share the limelight with *The General*. A 1967 poll of film historians and critics about the best comedy of all time, had *The Gold Rush* at no. 1, followed by *The General* and *Modern Times* (1936).[190] A survey of critics and historians conducted in the late 1970s to determine the 'most important' American films placed *The General* at no. 8 and *The Gold Rush* at no. 9.[191] Perhaps most importantly, in *Sight & Sound*'s 1962 survey of international critical opinion about the best films of all time, *The General* was at no. 21 (jointly with several other titles), behind *City Lights* (1931) and

The Gold Rush (jointly at no. 17).[192] In the magazine's next poll in 1972, *The General* was in eighth place, and in 1982 it was at no. 10.[193] On both occasions, *The General* was the only American film from the silent era in the top ten, and Chaplin's two (largely) non-talking films from the sound era – *City Lights* and *Modern Times* – did not make it into the top ten either. As I have suggested in the Introduction, since then, *The General* has arguably become the most popular and most highly acclaimed American movie from the silent period. The film is thus both closely associated with a bygone era and perceived as a timeless classic.

My intention for this book has been to offer new insights into the story, themes and style of *The General*, revealing complexities behind the film's apparent simplicity, and tragedy behind its apparent happy ending, and also to situate it in the historical context in which it was conceived, produced, marketed to a mass audience and first engaged with by critics and regular cinemagoers. While my account hopefully includes lots of material that readers (even avid fans and dedicated scholars) were not previously familiar with, it is by no means intended to be definitive. Instead, I hope that it can serve as an invitation, encouraging readers to turn, or return, to the voluminous literature on Keaton, to dig deeper into the archives, and to immerse themselves once again in *The General* and Keaton's other films, in the process gaining both enjoyment from, and further insights into, the work of this unique film-maker and performer.

Notes

1 See, for example, the article 'Comedian Fire Fighter' and a small untitled item (in the fourth column) on the 'Good Features' page of the press book; most of its pages do not have numbers and in subsequent endnotes I will only provide the article's title. I am very grateful to Kevin Brownlow for giving me access to the copy of this press book in his personal collection, which from now on I will refer to as KBC. The phrase 'comedy spectacle' is also used, for example, by the *New York Evening Post* on 5 February 1927; untitled and unpaginated clipping in folder MFL n.c. 1545, Performing Arts Research Center (PARC), New York Public Library at Lincoln Center, New York.

2 Drew Gilpin Faust, *This Republic of Suffering: Death and the American Civil War* (New York: Knopf, 2008), p. xi.

3 Ibid., pp. xi, 274.

4 Ibid., p. xii.

5 Cf. Melvyn Stokes, *D. W. Griffith's* The Birth of a Nation: A History of 'The Most Controversial Motion Picture of All Time' (Oxford: Oxford University Press, 2007), and Linda Williams, *Playing the Race Card: Melodramas of Black and White from Uncle Tom to O. J. Simpson* (Princeton, NJ: Princeton University Press, 2001), chs. 3 and 5.

6 *The General* is at no. 18. Charles Chaplin's *City Lights* (1931) is at no. 11, but this film, while without spoken dialogue, was in fact made – with a synchronised soundtrack (including music and sound effects) – *after* the American film industry had converted to sound. See 'AFI's 100 Years … 100 Movies – 10th Anniversary Edition'. Available at: <http://www.afi.com/100years/movies10.aspx>; last accessed 26 March 2015.

7 'The Top 100 Films' and 'Top 10s by Decade', *Sight & Sound* vol. 22 no. 9, September 2012, pp. 56, 59.

8 *City Lights* and Chaplin's *Modern Times* (1936) also came ahead of *The General*, but although *Modern Times* does mostly without spoken dialogue, it was, like *City Lights*, made with a synchronised soundtrack, including sound effects and some spoken words; 'Top 250 Movies as Voted by Regular IMDb Users'. Available at: <http://www.imdb.com/chart/top?ref_=chttp_q12>; last accessed 18 August 2015.

9 Review of *The General*, *Variety*, 9 February 1927, p. 16.

10 Katherine Zimmermann, 'Much Ado About Nothing in *General*', *New York Telegram*, 7 February 1927, MFL n.c. 1545, PARC.

11 Dorothy Herzog, Review of *The General*, *New York Mirror*, 7 February 1927, MFL n.c. 1545, PARC.

12 Review of *The General*, *New York Telegraph*, 7 February 1927, MFL n.c. 1545, PARC.

13 'Comedians and "Hamlet" Complex Again', *New York Sun*, 8 February 1927, MFL n.c. 1545, PARC.

14 Palmer Smith, Review of *The General*, *New York Evening World*, 8 February 1927, MFL n.c. 1545, PARC.

15 Robert Sherwood, Review of *The General*, *Life*, 24 February 1927, p. 26.

16 Review of *The General*, *Reeland Review*, 11 February 1927, MFL n.c. 1545, PARC.

17 Review of *The General*, *New York Post*, 7 February 1927, MFL n.c. 1545, PARC.

18 Review of *The General*, *Motion Picture Classic*, April 1927, p. 8.

19 Mildred Martin, 'Buster Keaton in *The General* at Fox', *Philadelphia Inquirer*, 29 March 1927, clippings file on *The General*, PARC.

20 Joe Keaton, 'The Cyclone Baby', *Photoplay*, May 1927, pp. 98, 125–6.

21 Ibid., p. 125.

22 Ibid.

23 Ibid.

24 See Jack Dragga's filmography in Marion Meade, *Buster Keaton: Cut to the Chase* (New York: HarperCollins, 1995), pp. 315–28.

25 While the press book for *The General* failed to mention Joe Keaton's presence in the film, he did receive some attention elsewhere; see, for example, 'Buster Keaton's Father in *The General*', *New York Telegraph*, 19 January 1927, clippings file on *The General*, PARC. The press book included two articles on Keaton's stage career ('Buster Keaton Tumbled to Fame' and 'Star of *The General* Came from Kansas') and another on the beginnings of his film career ('How I Broke into the Movies').

26 This paragraph and the next one are based on Peter Krämer, 'Battered Child: Buster Keaton's Stage Performance and Vaudeville Stardom in the Early 1900s', *New Review of Film and Television Studies* vol. 5 no. 3, December 2007, pp. 253–67; Peter Krämer, 'A Slapstick Comedian at the Crossroads: Buster Keaton, the Theater, and the Movies in 1916/17', *Theatre History Studies* vol. 17, 1997, pp. 133–46; and Peter Krämer, 'The Making of a Comic Star: Buster Keaton and *The Saphead*', in Kristine Brunovska

Karnick and Henry Jenkins (eds), *Classical Hollywood Comedy* (New York: Routledge, 1995), pp. 190–210, 376–83.

27 See the filmography in Meade, *Buster Keaton*, pp. 317–29.

28 Tom Dardis, *Keaton: The Man Who Wouldn't Lie Down* (New York: Scribner's, 1979), p. 148; Meade, *Buster Keaton*, p. 174.

29 There are no editing credits before *The General*, but from then until 1928, J. Sherman Kell, who may well have also worked on the earlier features, was credited as editor.

30 Later on, Buster Keaton's younger sister Louise would work as a stunt double on the final release of Buster Keaton Productions, *Steamboat Bill, Jr.* (1928).

31 This film is considered lost, but on the basis of contemporary reviews, Jim Kline offers a description in *The Complete Films of Buster Keaton* (New York: Citadel, 1993), pp. 39–40.

32 Joe Keaton also appeared in *Out West* (1918), without, however, getting involved in any mock fights with his son.

33 In *Convict 13*, Joe Keaton plays a fellow prisoner.

34 Unusually, there would be neither fathers nor grandfathers in *College* (1927), while in *Steamboat Bill, Jr.* the protagonist's romance is blocked by both his own and the girl's father.

35 Dardis, *Keaton*, p. 122; Meade, *Buster Keaton*, pp. 153, 159–60.

36 Cf. Krämer, 'Slapstick Comedian at the Crossroads', pp. 139–41, 145. The remainder of this paragraph, as well as the next one, largely draws on material from this essay and Krämer, 'Making of a Comic Star'.

37 Richard Koszarski, *An Evening's Entertainment: The Age of the Silent Feature Picture, 1915–1928* (Berkeley: University of California Press, 1999), pp. 116, 262, 281–3.

38 Dardis, Keaton, p. 40; Meade, *Buster Keaton*, p. 73.

39 Cf. Tino Balio, *United Artists: The Company Built by the Stars* (Madison: University of Wisconsin Press, 1976), pp. 52–7.

40 Ibid., p. 68; Neal Gabler, *An Empire of Their Own: How the Jews Invented Hollywood* (London: W. H. Allen, 1989), pp. 112–13.

41 David Bordwell, Janet Staiger and Kristin Thompson, *The Classical Hollywood Cinema: Film Style and Mode of Production to 1960* (London: Routledge and Kegan Paul, 1985), pp. 134–9; also see ch. 13.

42 Ibid., pp. 117–27, 139–40.

43 This paragraph is based on Buster Keaton with Charles Samuels, *My Wonderful World of Slapstick* (New York: Da Capo, 1982, originally published in 1960), pp. 123–78; Rudi Blesh, *Keaton* (New York: Collier, 1971, originally published in 1966), chs. 14–29; Dardis, *Keaton*, chs. 4–7; Meade, *Buster Keaton*, chs. 9–15; as well as the interviews collected in Kevin W. Sweeney (ed.), *Buster Keaton: Interviews* (Jackson: University Press of Mississippi, 2007). In addition, I draw on material relating specifically to the making of *The General*, which is referenced and discussed in some detail below.

44 Keaton received no directorial credit for *College* and *Steamboat Bill, Jr.*

45 See Chapter 7.

46 Incorporation record for the Comique Film Corporation, no. 1306-83, Bureau of Incorporation, Albany, New York; Dardis, *Keaton*, p. 114.

47 A copy of this contract is included in the KBC.

48 Below I indicate how one can calculate the profit each film made for Buster Keaton Productions. I would estimate combined profits to have been in the region of $800,000, so that Keaton's share was $200,000 – that is, about $50,000 more than the salary he was paid during the three years in question.

49 Ben J. Wattenberg (ed.), *The Statistical History of the United States* (New York: Basic Books, 1976), p. 165.

50 Koszarski, *Evening's Entertainment*, p. 116.

51 This review can be found on the right-hand side of the 'A Good Feature and Reviews' page.

52 See Krämer, 'Making of a Comic Star', pp. 190–210, 376–83.

53 Krämer, 'Battered Child', p. 258.

54 'How Did He Get It in California?', *New York Morning Telegraph*, 16 January 1921, KBC.

55 This press book can be found in the KBC.

56 This press book can be found on MFL n.c. 189, no. 12 (microfilm *ZAN* T8, reel 32), PARC. The film is often referred to as 'The Three Ages', perhaps because this is the title Raymond Rohauer used when re-releasing it (with newly designed credits).

57 See the annual box-office charts in Koszarski, *Evening's Entertainment*, p. 33.

58 It is also worth noting that in the short films he made with Arbuckle and in his own two-reelers, Keaton had regularly, but by no means always, donned a costume made up of a flat pork-pie hat, a shirt with clip-on tie, suspenders (usually covered by a vest) and oversized shoes. This outfit was used only rarely in his features.

59 Review of *The Navigator*, *Wid's Weekly*, 11 October 1924, and untitled article, *New York Sun*, 25 October 1924, both on MFL n.c. 1473, PARC.

60 'Buster Keaton in *Go West* Strives for Tragic Role', *New York Herald Tribune*, 26 October 1925, MFL n.c. 1534, PARC.

61 Koszarski, *Evening's Entertainment*, p. 33.

62 Tom Dardis, *Harold Lloyd: The Man on the Clock* (New York: Penguin, 1984), pp. 142, 155, 166, 179.

63 Rental figures are contained in a document from the Sears Correspondence 1941–50 in the United Artists Collection (UAC) at the State Historical Society of Wisconsin at Madison. Tino Balio kindly provided me with a photocopy of this document.

64 Dardis, *Keaton*, pp. 113, 126, 133–4.

65 Review of *Our Hospitality*, *New York Times*, 10 December 1923, Part 1, p. 20.

66 Mordaunt Hall, Review of *Battling Butler*, *New York Times*, 23 August 1926, Part 1, p. 9.

67 Review of *Go West*, *New York Evening Post*, 26 October 1925, MFL n.c. 1534, PARC.

68 Review of *Battling Butler*, *New York Telegraph*, 29 August 1926, MFL n.c. 1473, PARC.

69 Review of *Go West*, *New York Herald Tribune*, 26 October 1925, MFL n.c. 1534, PARC.

70 Review of *Go West*, *New York Telegram*, 26 October 1925, MFL n.c. 1534, PARC.

71 Reviews of *Battling Butler* in unidentified paper, 24 September 1926, and in the *Los Angeles Express*, 30 August 1926, both in MFL n.c. 1473, PARC.

72 Review of *The Navigator*, *New York World*, 19 October 1924, MFL n.c. 1473, PARC.

73 The KBC contains a copy of this contract.

74 See, for example, Sweeney, *Buster Keaton: Interviews*, pp. 52, 131, 186–7; and Keaton, *My Wonderful World of Slapstick*, p. 173.

75 Dardis (*Keaton*, p. 123) shares this assumption. The results of his calculations of the films' profitability are comparable to the one I propose here, although he arrives at his conclusions in a different manner.

76 Cf. Joel W. Finler, *The Hollywood Story* (London: Wallflower Press, 2003), pp. 41–2; and Koszarski, *Evening's Entertainment*, p. 85.

77 See the Eddie Mannix ledger, which provides financial data on all of MGM's in-house productions (thus, unfortunately, excluding films made by other companies such as Buster Keaton Productions) from 1924 to 1948. It is available as a microfiche supplement to H. Mark Glancy, 'MGM Film Grosses, 1924–1948: The Eddie Mannix Ledger', *Historical Journal of Film, Radio and Television* vol. 12 no. 2, 1992, pp. 127–43. For Glancy's calculation of seasonal averages, see p. 130.

78 Ibid., p. 130. I have adjusted Glancy's figures for the 1924–5 season to account for the highly anomalous performance of *Ben-Hur*.

79 I have calculated this figure from ibid. Cf. John Sedgwick, 'Richard B. Jewell's RKO Film Grosses, 1929–51: The C. J. Trevlin Ledger: A Comment', *Historical Journal of Film, Radio and Television* vol. 14 no. 1, 1994, p. 52.
80 Dardis, *Keaton*, p. 113.
81 This calculation assumes that domestic rentals came in well before income from foreign markets, so that the advance would all be recouped from the former.
82 Metro/MGM, by comparison, earned $490,000 ($310,000 plus $180,000) from each film, yet for each it had paid a $200,000 advance and the distribution costs (probably over $200,000), leaving less than $100,000 profit.
83 *Variety*, 27 August 1924, p. 26.
84 Dardis, *Keaton*, pp. 113, 126, 133–4.
85 Review of *The Navigator*, *New York Herald Tribune*, 13 October 1924, MFL n.c. 1528, PARC.
86 Unidentified review of *Go West*, 27 October 1925, MFL n.c. 1534, PARC. In addition to the divisiveness of Keaton's on-screen performance, his reluctance to present himself smilingly off screen – for example, in publicity photographs or during personal appearances – may also have alienated people. See, for example, 'Betcha He Doesn't Even Crack a Smile for [His Sons] Buster Jr. and Little Robert Keaton', *New York Daily News*, 14 March 1925, MFL n.c. 1530, PARC. Also cf. Krämer, 'Making of a Comic Star', pp. 209–10.
87 While the huge cost of the production is mentioned in almost all articles, it is particularly foregrounded in the following headline: '$1,000,000

Comedies Coming: Buster Keaton, Who Spent $500,000 on His Own, *The General*, Foresees Higher Cost of Laugh Production'.
88 See Chapter 2.
89 See especially the articles 'Actor in Keaton Film Remembers '65', 'Keaton Knocked Down by Explosion in Film', 'Keaton Picked Soldiers for Soldier Parts' and 'Buster Keaton Helped N.G.O. [National Guard of Oregon] Recruiting'.
90 See 'Keaton Film Based on Historical Fact' and 'Historical Accuracy in Keaton Picture'.
91 See especially '$1,000,000 Comedies Coming', 'Historical Accuracy in Keaton Picture', 'Ever Ride a High-Wheeled Bicycle?' and 'Keaton Worked Six Months before Filming a Scene'.
92 See '*The General* Made Spectators Hysterical', 'Original of "The General" Preserved in Tennessee', 'Cleared the Track for "The General"' and 'Keaton's Locomotives Not from a Toy Shop'.
93 Dardis, *Keaton*, pp. 113, 126, 133–4.
94 Robert Sherwood, Review of *The Navigator*, *Life*, 6 November 1924, MFL n.c. 1473, PARC.
95 Review of *The Navigator*, *New York Sun*, 13 October 1924, MFL n.c. 1528, PARC.
96 Unidentified clipping dated 16 August 1924, MFL n.c. 1473, PARC.
97 Buster Keaton, 'What Are the Six Ages of Comedy', *The Truth about the Movies* (Los Angeles: Hollywood Publishers, 1924), p. 441.
98 'Buster Keaton, in *Go West*, Strives for Tragic Role'.
99 'Counting the Comedy Cost', *New York Telegram*, 30 October 1925, MFL n.c. 1534, PARC.

100 Review of *Go West*, *New York Evening World*, 26 October 1925, MFL n.c. 1534, PARC.

101 Koszarski, *Evening's Entertainment*, p. 33.

102 'Keaton Brings 1830 America to the Screen', *Radford Journal*, 22 August 1924, MFL n.c. 1473, PARC.

103 Ibid.

104 Review of *Our Hospitality*, *New York Times*, 10 December 1923.

105 Review of *Our Hospitality*, *Variety*, 13 December 1923, p. 22.

106 Ibid.

107 See Glenn Mitchell, *A–Z of Silent Film Comedy: An Illustrated Companion* (London: B. T. Batsford, 1998), p. 115. *Hands Up!* was indeed later mentioned favourably in reviews of *The General*; see, for example, Sherwood, Review of *The General*, and 'Comedians and "Hamlet" Complex Again'.

108 Romances between supporters of the Confederacy and of the Union were a common element in Civil War movies, including *The Birth of a Nation*. Cf. Evelyn Ehrlich, 'The Civil War in Early Film: Origin and Development of a Genre', *Southern Quarterly: A Journal of the History of the South* vol. 19 nos. 3–4, 1981, pp. 70–82; and Eileen Bowser, *The Transformation of Cinema, 1907–1915* (Berkeley: University of California Press, 1990), pp. 177–9. According to these and other sources, the heyday of the Civil War film was the early to mid-1910s, whereas there were comparatively few films in this genre in the 20s. Also see Melvyn Stokes, 'The Civil War in the Movies', in Susan-Mary Grant and Peter J. Parish (eds), *Legacy of Disunion: The Enduring Significance of the American Civil War* (Baton Rouge: Louisiana State University Press, 2003), pp. 66–9.

109 Meade, *Buster Keaton*, p. 161; Kevin Brownlow, 'The D. W. Griffith of Comedy', in John Boorman and Walter Donahue (eds), *Projections 4½* (London: Faber, 1995), p. 293; George Wead, 'The Great Locomotive Chase', *American Film* vol. 2 no. 9, July–August 1977, p. 20.

110 Dardis, *Harold Lloyd*, p. 209.

111 Blesh, *Keaton*, pp. 129–30.

112 Brownlow, 'D. W. Griffith of Comedy', p. 301.

113 Ibid., pp. 301–2, and interview with Marion Mack in Richard J. Anobile (ed.), *Buster Keaton's* The General (New York: Darien House, 1975), p. 14.

114 Anobile, *Buster Keaton's* The General, p. 14.

115 Untitled articles in *Hollywood News*, 20 January 1926; *Los Angeles News*, 25 February 1926; and *Hollywood Review*, 19 March 1926 – all on MFL n.c. 1473, PARC.

116 This paragraph is mainly based on Brownlow, 'D. W. Griffith of Comedy', pp. 289–312, which in turn is based on interviews, site visits and contemporary reports in the local press. Also see Wead, 'Great Locomotive Chase', pp. 20–4; Meade, *Buster Keaton*, pp. 162–9; John Bengtson, *Silent Echoes: Discovering Early Hollywood through the Films of Buster Keaton* (Santa Monica, CA: Santa Monica Press, 2000), pp. 180–98; and various articles from the press book: 'Original of "The General" Preserved in Tennessee', 'Comedian Fire Fighter', '$1,000,000 Comedies Coming', 'Cleared the Track for "The General"', 'Three Thousand People in Buster Keaton Comedy',

'*The General* Made Spectators Hysterical', 'Buster Keaton Built a Town for Movie' and 'Buster Keaton Helped N.G.O. Recruiting'.

117 Dardis, *Keaton*, p. 145.

118 William Pittenger, *Capturing a Locomotive: A History of Secret Service in the Late War* (Washington, DC: The National Tribune, 1885; later editions carried the title *The Great Locomotive Chase*). I am using the original version as reproduced by Project Gutenberg, release date 17 July 2011, ebook no. 36752. Available at: <https://www.gutenberg.org/files/36752/36752-h/36752-h.htm>; last accessed 6 November 2015. Pittenger had written about the Andrews raid in several earlier publications, including a short 1863 book entitled *Daring and Suffering: A History of the Great Railway Adventure*. For previous discussions of Pittenger's work and its relationship to *The General*, see, for example, E. Rubinstein, *Filmguide to* The General (Bloomington: Indiana University Press, 1973), pp. 17–18; and Wolfgang Karrer, 'Buster Keaton's *The General*: Zur Fiktionalisierung des amerikanischen Bürgerkriegs', *Anglistik & Englischunterricht* vol. 13, April 1981, pp. 83–7.

119 Pittenger, *Capturing a Locomotive*, p. 6.

120 Ibid., pp. 35–6.

121 Ibid., pp. 61–2.

122 Ibid., p. 238.

123 Ibid., pp. 47–8.

124 Ibid., p. 122.

125 Ibid., p. 129.

126 See, for example, ibid., pp. 268–71.

127 Ibid., p. 170.

128 Ibid., p. 174.

129 Ibid., p. 238; also see, for example, p. 324.

130 Thomas Cripps, 'The Absent Presence in American Civil War Films', *Historical Journal of Film, Radio and Television* vol. 14 no. 4, 1994, p. 371.

131 Pittenger, *Capturing a Locomotive*, p. 70.

132 Ibid., p. 96.

133 Ibid., p. 85.

134 Ibid., pp. 85–6.

135 Ibid., p. 86.

136 Ibid., p. 87.

137 Ibid., p. 88.

138 Ibid., p. 99.

139 Ibid., p. 100.

140 Ibid., pp. 103–5.

141 Ibid., pp. 112–13.

142 The film also foregrounds the raiders' belief that they cannot stop to fight the Texas. Only able to see the front of the train, Andrews says: 'I'm afraid they have us greatly outnumbered.'

143 Pittenger, *Capturing a Locomotive*, pp. 123–5.

144 Ibid., p. 114.

145 Ibid., p. 118; also see pp. 91, 105.

146 Ibid., pp. 118–19.

147 The version of *The General* I am referring to is on the 2004 MK2 DVD of the film. All the timings in this book relate to this DVD.

148 See, for example, Sweeney, *Buster Keaton: Interviews*, p. 50, also pp. 23, 39; and Keaton, *My Wonderful World of Slapstick*, p. 175.

149 Blesh, *Keaton*, pp. 251–4; Dardis, *Keaton*, p. 109; Meade, *Buster Keaton*, pp. 147–8; Sweeney, *Buster Keaton: Interviews*, pp. 23–4, 39–40, 59–60, 82–3.

150 Cf. Ehrlich, 'Civil War in Early Film'; Bowser, *Transformation of Cinema*, pp. 177–9; Stokes, 'Civil War in the Movies'; Cripps,

'Absent Presence in American Civil War Films'. In later interviews, Keaton repeatedly stated that it had been an unwritten rule that the Confederates should not be the villains; see Sweeney, *Buster Keaton: Interviews*, pp. 137, 206, 227.

151 Bordwell, Staiger and Thompson, *Classical Hollywood Cinema*, p. 16.

152 Review of *The General* in the third column of the 'A Good Feature and Reviews' page, and 'Keaton Worked Six Months before Filming One Scene'.

153 'Keaton's Laugh Feast Coming to …'.

154 '$1,000,000 Comedies Coming'.

155 Bengtson, *Silent Echoes*, pp. 183, 193. Also see, for example, the Wikipedia entry on *The General*. Available at: <https://en.wikipedia.org/wiki/The_General_(1926_film)>; last accessed 26 August 2015.

156 In this version of the Civil War, then, Chattanooga was taken by the Union army already in April 1862; in reality, this did not happen until September 1863. It is perhaps worth mentioning that there is a famous 'Battle of Chattanooga' which took place at the end of November 1863; this was the result of a successful Union offensive in the vicinity of Chattanooga.

157 Cf. Louis Giannetti, *Understanding Movies. 5th Edition* (Englewood Cliffs, NJ: Prentice-Hall, 1990), pp. 306–9; and Rubinstein, *Filmguide to* The General, pp. 2–3.

158 See, for example, Rubinstein, *Filmguide to* The General, pp. 22–64; Giannetti, *Understanding Movies*, pp. 306–9; Noël Carroll, *Comedy Incarnate: Buster Keaton, Physical Humor, and Bodily Coping* (Malden, MA: Blackwell, 2007), pp. 158–74;

and Daniel Moews, *Keaton: The Silent Features Close Up* (Berkeley: University of California Press, 1977), pp. 212–45.

159 Roscoe McGowan, Review of *The General*, *New York Daily News*, undated; Review of *The General*, *New York Herald Tribune*, 8 February 1927; and Review of *The General*, *New York Telegraph*, 7 February 1927 – all on MFL n.c. 1545, PARC.

160 'Historical Accuracy in Keaton Picture', 'Buster Keaton's New Film Coming to …' and 'Ever Ride a High-Wheeled Bicycle?'.

161 Keaton first developed this characterisation in Metro's *The Saphead*.

162 For a similarly pessimistic reading of the film's ending, see, for example, Gerald Mast, '*The Gold Rush* and *The General*', *Cinema Journal* vol. 9, 1970, pp. 28–30.

163 For a wonderfully perceptive and highly systematic discussion of Johnnie's actions and the various kinds of gags they give rise to, see Carroll, *Comedy Incarnate*, ch. 1. My analysis of *The General* owes a great debt to Carroll's study.

164 For a fascinating discussion of the thematic relevance of style in *The General* and other Keaton features, see ibid., ch. 2.

165 For an important revisionist analysis of the depiction of women in *The General* and other Keaton features, see Barbara E. Savedoff, 'Reconsidering Buster Keaton's Heroines', *Philosophy and Literature* vol. 21, 1997, pp. 77–90.

166 Untitled article, *New York Evening Post*, 5 February 1927, MFL n.c. 1545, PARC.

167 Before this American premiere, there had been a world premiere in Tokyo on 31 December 1926; Meade, *Buster Keaton*, p. 328.

168 The information in this paragraph is taken from the Capitol programme, which is contained in the clippings file on *The General* at PARC.

169 The Capitol programme states that the first full programme of the day started at 2 p.m. and the second at 4 p.m. Since the screening of *The General* started at 2.38 p.m., it lasted 82 minutes *minus* at least ten minutes allowing for thousands of people to exit to the music of the organ and for the next audience to come in. Thus, the projection speed appears to have been quite high (higher, indeed, than the 25 fps on the DVD I have been using for this book; on that DVD, the film runs for 75 minutes 27 seconds). Daniel Moews has used a music cue sheet for *The General* (that is, a guide to the music that was to be played for each scene) to estimate that the film's running time was only 62 minutes, which would be equivalent to a projection speed of over 30 fps. Thus, the version we watch today does not run fast enough when compared to how audiences experienced the film in 1927! See Moews, *Keaton*, pp. 323–5; cf. Koszarski, *Evening's Entertainment*, pp. 58–9.

170 Cf. the programme for the Metropolitan Theatre contained in the same folder as the one for the Capitol; also see Koszarski, *Evening's Entertainment*, pp. 30–1, 41–54.

171 Mordaunt Hall, Review of *The General*, *New York Times*, 8 February 1927, Part 1, p. 21.

172 Martin, 'Buster Keaton in *The General* at Fox'.

173 See the document from the Sears Correspondence 1941–50, UAC, cited in n. 63.

174 This contract from December 1926 is in the O'Brien Legal Files, UAC.

175 Cf. Glancy, 'MGM Film Grosses', p. 130, and Sedgwick, 'Richard B. Jewell's RKO Film Grosses', pp. 55–8.

176 See Dardis, *Keaton*, p. 149, and the document from the Sears Correspondence, UAC.

177 Ibid.

178 For a brief overview, see Donald Crafton, *The Talkies: American Cinema's Transition to Sound, 1926–1931* (Berkeley: University of California Press, 1999), pp. 8–18.

179 Dardis, *Keaton*, pp. 152–6.

180 Ibid., p. 158; there is a copy of this contract in the KBC.

181 Dardis, *Keaton*, pp. 153–5.

182 Stokes, *D. W. Griffith's* The Birth of a Nation, pp. 242–9.

183 Matthew Solomon, *The Gold Rush* (London: BFI, 2015), pp. 72–7.

184 Meade, *Buster Keaton*, pp. 248–60; Moews, *Keaton*, pp. 327–30.

185 Paul Warshow, 'More Is Less: Comedy and Sound', *Film Quarterly* vol. 31 no. 1, Autumn 1977, pp. 39–41.

186 Blesh, *Keaton*, p. 369; Sweeney, *Buster Keaton*, pp. 147–8.

187 Cf. Sweeney, *Buster Keaton: Interviews*.

188 Cobbett S. Steinberg, *Film Facts* (New York: Facts on File, 1980), p. 232.

189 Solomon, *Gold Rush*, pp. 80–1.

190 Steinberg, *Film Facts*, pp. 185–6.

191 Koszarski, *Evening's Entertainment*, pp. 318–19. For further poll results, see Steinberg, *Film Facts*, pp. 141–4, 186–7.

192 Steinberg, *Film Facts*, p. 127.

193 Ian Christie, 'Chronicle of a Fall Foretold', *Sight & Sound* vol. 22 no. 9, September 2012, p. 57.

Credits

The General
USA/1926

Directed by
Buster Keaton
Clyde Bruckman
Written by
Buster Keaton
Clyde Bruckman
Adapted by
Al Boasberg
Charles [Henry] Smith
Photographed by
Dev [Devereaux]
Jennings
Bert Haines

© Joseph M. Schenck
Production Company
Joseph M. Schenck
presents
a United Artists
production

Lighting Effects
Denver Harmon
Technical Director
Fred Gabourie

uncredited
Based on William
Pittenger, *Capturing a
Locomotive: A History of
Secret Service in the Late
War* (1885)
Production Company
Buster Keaton
Productions, Inc.
Producer
Joseph M. Schenck
**2nd Unit Director
(Battle Scenes)**
Glen Cavender

Assistant Director
Harry Barnes
**Assistant Director
(Oregon)**
Edward Hearn
Script Supervisor
Christine Francis
Casting Director
Harry Barnes
Production Supervisor
Lou Anger
Production Manager
Fred Gabourie
Production Coordinator
Harry Brand
**Assistant Production
Coordinator**
John W. Considine Jr
Unit/Location Manager
Bert E. Jackson
Production Secretary
Betty Cavender
**Production Accountant
(Los Angeles)**
Lou Anger
**Production Accountant
(Oregon)**
Wesley G. Gilmour
Camera Operators
Dal Clawson
William Piltz
Camera Assistant
Harry J. Wild
Camera Technician
Elmer Ellsworth
Chief Electrician
Ed Levy
Key Grip
Frank Barnes
Still Photographer
Byron Houck
Publicity Photographer
Melbourne Spurr

**Special Effects/
Munitions**
Jack Little
Editor
Buster Keaton
Assistant Editors
Sherman Kell
Harry Barnes
Art Director
Fred Gabourie
Set Decorator
Harry Roselotte
Chief Draughtsman
Billy Wood
Property Master
Bert E. Jackson
Production Buyer
Al Gilmour
Property Assistant
Mike Graves
Construction Foreman
Frank Barnes
Carpenter
Jack Coyle
**Bridge/Dam
Construction**
H. L. Jennings
Bridge/Dam Contractor
George E. Potter
Bridge Timber Crew
William Ernshaw
Wardrobe
J. K. Pitcairn
Wardrobe Assistants
Bennie Hubbel
Fred Carlton Ryle
Costumes
Western Costume
Company
Make-up
J. K. Pitcairn

Make-up Assistants
Fred Carlton Ryle
Bennie Hubbel
**Stunt Double
(Tom Moran)**
Earl Mohan
**Horses/Mules
Supplied by**
Dee Wright
Chief Mechanic
Fred Wright
Train Engineer
Jack Dempster
Train Brakeman
Fred A. Lowry
**Railroad Assistance
(Oregon)**
L. L. Graham
Bob Holmes
Catering
George E. Potter
Anderson & Middleton
Chef
Ralph Land
**Assistant to
Buster Keaton**
Willie Riddle
Buster Keaton's Cook
Viola Riddle
First Aid
Dr Axley
Dr Frost
Unit Publicist
Harry Brand

CAST
Buster Keaton
Johnnie Gray
Marion Mack
Annabelle Lee
Glen Cavender
Captain Anderson

Jim Farley
General Thatcher
Frederick Vroom
a Southern general
Charles [Henry] Smith
Annabelle's father
Frank Barnes
Annabelle's brother
Joe Keaton
Mike Donlin
Tom Nawn
three Union generals

uncredited
Jackie Lowe
boy who follows Johnny
Al St John
officer on horseback
Frank Hagney
Confederate recruiter
Jack Dempster
Jimmy Bryant
Budd Fine
Ray Hanford
Al Hanson
Anthony Harvey
Ross McCutcheon
Tom Moran
Charles Phillips
Red Rial
Ray Thomas
Red Thompson
raiders
Eddie Foster
Union railroad fireman
Devereaux Jennings
Union general giving
command to cross bridge
Edward Hearn
Union officer
Ronald Gilstrap
Harold Terry
John Wilson

Henry Baird
Joe Bricher
Keith Fennell
Hilliard Karr
Louis Lewyn
Billy Lynn
James Walsh
Sergeant Bukowski
C. C. Cruson
Union and
Confederate soldiers

Filmed from 8 June to
25 September 1926
mainly on location in
Cottage Grove, Eugene,
McKenzie River and Row
River (Oregon); also at
the Buster Keaton Studio
in Hollywood, and in
Santa Monica (California).
Budget: $415,000. 35mm;
1.33:1; black & white
(Sepiatone); silent.

US theatrical release by
United Artists in New
York City (New York)
on 5 February 1927.
Length: 7,500 feet
UK theatrical release in
London by Allied Artists
Corporation Ltd on
17 January 1927.
Certificate: U.
Length: 7,100 feet
UK theatrical re-release
by Park Circus on
24 January 2014

Credits compiled by
Julian Grainger